TABLE OF CONTENTS

This book is dedicated to my husband, Doug, and children, Debbie, kim, Allison & David.

I am most thankful for their patience and willingness to be guinea pigs!

A special thanks to Dena and Ernie Smith, whose faith and encouragement prompted me to write this book.

The recipes in this book are old family favorites converted to microwave recipes, or given to me by cooking class customers, family & friends.

For success in using your micro-wave oven, especially if you are a new "microwaver", read-ing the introduction is very important.

Introduction

The recipes in this book were tested in a 700 watt oven. Lower wattage units may want a little more time.

Remember: You're better off to under-cook things and add time if you need to.

1: How a microwave oven operates

2: Utensils you can use

3: Utensils you'll want to purchase

4: Covers to use

5: Converting

6: Reheating

7: Carry-over cooking time

8: Power levels

9: Defrosting

1: <u>How a microwave oven operates</u>:

They all plug into a three - prong (grounded) outlet, & draw as much power as a four- slice toaster (1300 - 1500 watts) The power comes into a transformer which boosts the power to the magnatron tube. * This tube is as important as the picture tube is in your T.V.! It produces radiowaves at a rate of 2½ billion times per second ..... & that's fast !!

The radiowaves travel along a wave guide & into the oven. You'll find that radiowaves pass through everything except metal. (This is why you can cook in paper, glass, ceramic, etc.) The only way you can keep the radiowaves in the oven, is to enclose them in a metal box. Your microwave oven has 4 metal sides (a metal screen in the window) & a metal top & bottom. If your oven has a creamy finish to the insides, tap it, & you'll see that it's painted metal and not plastic. Any glass or plastic parts inside your oven will have metal behind them.

Now..... we have the radiowaves

in a six-sided metal box; then what happens?? The radiowaves travel in a straight line, bounce off the metal walls & go to the water molecules in the food. *(If there are no water molecules in the oven, the radiowaves travel back up the wave guide & overheat the magnatron tube.) <u>That's why you must never operate the oven empty</u>!!! Like the picture tube in your T.V., it's a costly item to replace! When the radiowaves hit the water molecules, they start polarizing against each other like two magnets do, because both the radiowaves & the water molecules have a positive & a negative end. Now that we have them polarizing against each other, we realize that they are doing that at a rate of 2½ billion times per second, (That's how fast the radiowaves are transmitted.) At this speed, they are rubbing against each other, which causes friction, friction causes heat, and that's what cooks your food.

Now... isn't that simple ??!*!

2: <u>Utensils you can use</u>:

Because radiowaves pass through everything except metal, you can use anything <u>except</u> metal. But remember, the microwave oven doesn't get hot, but your food <u>does</u>! When you are using plastics or glass etc., make sure they are "microwave safe". This means they can tolerate the heat your food will reach & the heat of the steam. You'll find some plastics, like the margarine containers, will just buckle with the heat, & they could give off fumes you don't want!

3: <u>Utensils you'll want to purchase</u>:

There are many microwave accessories on the market. Depending on what you have in your kitchen, some will be more important than others.

A) <u>a browning grill</u>:
This is a dish designed to get hot in the microwave. You'll use this for browning any of your meats that cook

too fast to brown, and for cooking those foods that need a hot surface (fishcakes, pancakes, grilled sandwiches, eggs etc.) Follow manufacture's instructions for pre-heating.

B) <u>a meat rack</u>:

You will find you need a micro-wave meat rack for roasting all your meats. You will also use this rack for chicken pieces, canapés, sandwiches, baking cakes, etc.

c) <u>a kitchen scale</u>:

"ALMOST A MUST" for microwave cook-ing! If you have a kitchen scale, use it. If not, I recommend a "microwave" scale. You will find that just about everything that cooks in the microwave oven, cooks by weight. The microwave scale not only weighs your food, but also tells you how long it will take to cook.... what more could you ask for ??! ☺

D) <u>baking dishes</u>:

Most people have metal baking pans, but remember... metal is a "NO-NO" in the microwave oven! If you have glass baking dishes, GREAT... use them. You may find you'll want to purchase any of the following plastic baking dishes:

- an 8"-9" (1 Litre) cake pan for your 1-layer size cake.
- a bundt pan for your larger 2-layer size cakes.
- a muffin pan for muffins, & baking eggs for salads, sandwiches, or just eating. These can also be used for rice or salmon cakes, as well as making great containers for your stuffed tomatoes, onions or green peppers.

E) <u>batter bowl</u>:

These come in a couple of sizes. The handle, spout & shape of the bowl make it most useful for: measuring, mixing, cooking soup, rice, making jams & jellies, sauces, or just about any kitchen job!

4:   <u>Covers to use</u>:

Many people ask when to use plastic wrap & when to use wax paper. Follow this guide, thinking of the end product & what you want to achieve:

Plastic wrap: Some are better than others. I recommend one marked "microwave safe." Use plastic wrap whenever you want to steam anything. It works the same way as a glass lid. Use it (or your microwave safe lid) whenever you're doing vegetables, poaching fish, pot roasting etc. Because plastic wrap forms such a tight seal, turn a corner back to allow a steam vent. (This works better than just puncturing the top, as the slit often gets larger with steam pressure, you loose too much steam, & in some cases, this will dry out your food.)

Wax paper: Use wax paper whenever you are roasting. This cover sits loosely on top of the food, & will allow a lot of the excess steam to escape. Use it for roast chicken (whole or pieces) & some casseroles.

Paper towel: Paper towel has two main uses... whenever you are warming bread products, you should wrap them in paper towel. Bread products are very porous & heat very quickly. The moisture will evaporate & unless the bread is covered, the fan will send the moisture away. If you cover the bread with plastic wrap, the moisture will condense on the wrap & leave the bread product damp. However, the paper towel absorbs the moisture & leaves the bread moist. The other use for paper towel is when cooking bacon ... the paper towel absorbs the fat & spatters.

Aluminum foil: Aluminum foil is used for shielding. Remember that radio-waves pass through everything except metal. If there is an area of your food that is over-cooking, such as the legs on a turkey, or the thin area of an odd-shaped roast; put a small amount of aluminum foil on that part & the radiowaves will deflect off the foil & go to the area that needs more cooking. Some important rules of thumb when using foil are:

i) Don't cover more than 1/4 of the mass. The majority of the food should be exposed.

ii) Make sure the foil is snug, with no pieces sticking up.

iii) Make sure the foil isn't within 1" of the walls of the oven.

5:   <u>Converting</u>:

It's better to follow microwave recipes at first. You'll soon get to know the timings & covers to use. When you're ready to start converting, find a microwave recipe that is similar & adjust time & ingredients accordingly.

<u>Casseroles</u>:   You may want to pre-cook onions for casseroles, as sometimes the speed of cooking is so great, they don't always get a chance to soften. You'll also find that because of the speed of cooking, there won't be as much evap-oration of liquids. Depending on the casserole, you may want to cut back on some of the liquids.

<u>Cakes</u>: These are the trickiest to con-vert! Again, follow the microwave

recipes at first. You'll find the batter is thicker. Conventional cake recipes have extra moisture in them to allow for the evaporation that will take place in a 350° oven for 30-60 minutes. In a microwave oven the cooking time will be down to 4-14 minutes. The microwave oven is not hot, so you don't need that extra moisture. The general rule of thumb is to cut back the liquid of your conventional recipe by 1/4; (i.e.) if it calls for 1 cup of liquid, just add 3/4 cup. You'll also find that egg size may affect your cakes. Most recipes are done with medium sized eggs. Because farm eggs are so large, they add extra moisture & grade B eggs have extra moisture in them as well. I like to cover cakes with wax paper while cooking. Cook on full power. 8" (1L) — 4-7 minutes. Bundt pan size — 10-14 minutes.

6: Reheating:

There is no hard & fast rule I can give for reheating, as it really depends on the ingredients & how cold the food

INTRODUCTION

is. You'll have better results if you reheat on power level 8 or a med.-high
setting. This slows up the process, but
allows the heat to travel to the center of
the food, without overcooking the outside edges.

Guide:

one plate (reheat)	- 1-2 min; covered
one plate (cold-reheat)	- 2½-3½ min; covered
casserole (reheat)	- 4-6 min; covered
casserole (cold-reheat)	- 8-10 min; covered

7: <u>Carry-over cooking time</u> :

You'll find that nearly everything
that cooks in a microwave oven, finishes
cooking on the counter in 5-15 minutes
<u>AFTER</u> coming out of the oven. This is
called "standing time" or "carry-over
cooking time." DON'T be tempted, when
you check your vegetables, to "ZAP"
them some more! Give them the desig-
nated cooking time, allow 5-10 minutes
"carry-over cooking time," & then check
for doneness. Chances are they'll be
just right after standing!

8:   <u>Power levels</u>:

   Most microwave ovens today have variable power. Depending on the model you purchase, there may be anywhere from 1-10 power levels. Similar to the element dials on your conventional oven, you may have settings from 1-10, (10 being the highest heat down to 1 being the lowest heat.) i.e: if you had something boiling over on high, you would reduce the heat to 5 or a medium setting. Relate the variable power settings on your microwave oven to the element dials on your conventional oven.
   Basically, the power levels in a microwave oven are as follows :

<u>Full power</u>:
   - is the highest setting ; also referred to as "high" , "power level 10" or "100% power."

<u>Medium-High power</u>:
   - a medium-high setting <u>or</u> between "power levels 6-8 " or "60-80% power."

<u>Medium power</u>:
- also referred to as "½ power", "power level 5" or "50% power".

<u>Medium·Low power</u>:
- this can be your "defrost" cycle or "power levels 3-4" or "30-40% power."

<u>Low power</u>:
- this is the lowest setting on your dial; also referred to as "warm", or in some ovens "defrost", "power level 1", or "10% power."

9: <u>Defrosting</u>: (See also "TIPS" P. 63 & P. 94)

In most cases this is 30% power but in others it may be 50% power ... BUT... there is no reason why you can't defrost on a lower setting if you find your oven's defrost cycle too fast for certain foods.

<u>Defrost cycle</u>:

Basically, as the microwave oven defrosts, it warms up the outside edges of the food. It's those warm outside edges that melt the ice crystals. Towards the end of the defrost time, you may find that those warm outside edges will start cooking ... you can slow up this process by shutting the oven off, breaking away the cooked areas (ie. ground beef) or shielding those cooked areas with aluminum foil. (See P.13-14)

It is important to remember that everything that defrosts in the microwave oven should have a "HOLDING TIME" - after defrosting & before cooking. This allows the temperature to become uniform throughout. The holding time is equal to the defrost time. (i.e.) if it takes 15 minutes to defrost a roast ... you really shouldn't cook it for another 15 minutes.

READY?   SET?

LET'S

MICROWAVE   IT!

"HELPFUL TIMINGS"

Here are some basic timings.... all are on full power unless stated otherwise.

Apple; baked	2-2½ min./apple (cover)
Baby bottle; each	30-45 sec.
Bacon	½-1½ min./slice
Baked potato	4-6 min./potato
Butter; melted	45 sec.-1min./¼ lb.
Butter; softened	10-15 sec./¼ lb.
Casseroles; cooked ingredients	8-10 min./2qt (2L) size
Cocoa	1½-2 min./mug
Coffee; instant	2-2½ min./cup
Corn on the cob; in husk or wrapped	2-3 min./cob
Dinner plate; reheat	1-2 min. (covered)
Dinner plate; cold → reheat	2½-3½ min.(Level B: med.high)
Dinner rolls; in paper towel	10-15 sec. each
Dinner rolls; basket & paper towel	30-45 sec./½ dozen
Egg (1)	1-1½ min(Level B: med high)
Fish	4 min./lb. (6-8 min./kg.)
Ground beef	4-6 min./lb. (9-13 min./kg)
Hot dog; wiener & bun in napkin	25-35 sec. each
Muffin	10-15 sec. each
Pie	30-45 sec. each
Sandwich; in paper towel	30-45 sec. each
Soup	1½-2 min./bowl
Vegetables; above-ground	} 6-8 min./lb. (10-12 min./kg)
Vegetables; root (with ¼ cup water)	
Vegetables; canned (drain)	1-2 min./cup
Vegetables; blanched (covered)	3-4 min/lb (6-8 min./kg)
Water; boiling	2-3 min./cup

Appetizers

RUMAKI

-This is the nicest recipe for Rumaki I've had,
& I think the marinade makes it!

	IMPERIAL	METRIC
chicken livers	6	6
water chestnuts; optional	4	4
bacon slices	6	6
brown sugar	½ cup	125 mL
teriyaki sauce		

1:    Make up teriyaki sauce:

	IMPERIAL	METRIC
salad oil	¼ cup	50 mL
soy sauce	¼ cup	50 mL
ketchup	2 tbsp.	25 mL
vinegar	1 tbsp.	15 mL
pepper	¼ tsp.	1 mL
garlic cloves; crushed	2	2

Mix all ingredients together. Cut chicken
livers in half & the water chestnuts in 3.
Marinate them in teriyaki sauce for at
least 4 hours, (overnight is best) in the
refrigerator.

2:    Cut bacon in half & wrap 1 piece of liver
& 1 piece of water chestnut in bacon.
Secure with a toothpick & roll in brown
sugar.

3:    Arrange on meat rack & cover with paper
towel. Cook on full power for 5-7 minutes.

TAMMY'S SHRIMP MOLD

- This is so good you'll be tempted to eat half of it before you serve it!

	IMPERIAL	METRIC
gelatin	1 tbsp.	7 g
water	2 tbsp.	25 mL
tomato soup; condensed	½ (10 oz) can	½ (284 g) can
shrimp pieces	2 (6½ oz) cans	2 (195 g) cans
celery; diced	½ cup	125 mL
green onion; finely sliced	¼ cup	50 mL
mayonnaise	¾ cup	175 mL
Philadelphia cream cheese	4 oz.	113 g

1: Dissolve gelatin in water, in a small cup.
2: Heat tomato soup on full power for 35-45 seconds.
3: Combine shrimp, celery, onion, mayonnaise & cheese with the soup.
4: Add gelatin mixture to the soup mixture. Mix well. Pour into mold & refrigerate 2-3 hours, until set.

Get the flavour of cream cheese, without the calories, by using Neufchâtel cheese, a partly-skim cheese that tastes just like cream cheese.

TIP

Make toast shapes using cookie cutters
or by cutting toast into squares, triangles, or
rectangles. Top with any of the following
"nibbly" toppings:

SHRIMP:

	IMPERIAL	METRIC
margarine	½ cup	125 mL
Velveeta cheese; grated	½ lb.	250 g
shrimp; drained	1 (4oz.)can	1 (113g)can

1: Blend margarine, cheese & shrimp. Spread
  lightly on toast nibbles (above) or crackers. Too much makes spillovers!

2: Place on meat rack & heat on full power
  30-45 seconds.

CRAB:

	IMPERIAL	METRIC
crab meat	1 (6½ oz)can	1 (195g)can
green onion; sliced	1 tbsp.	15 mL
Swiss cheese; grated	½ cup	125 mL
mayonnaise	½ cup	125 mL
lemon juice	1 tsp.	5 mL
curry powder	¼ tsp.	1 mL

1: Blend crab meat, onion, cheese, mayonnaise, lemon juice & curry powder.
  Spread lightly, as above for shrimp.

2:   Place on meat rack & heat on full pow-
     er 30-45 seconds.

TUNA:

	IMPERIAL	METRIC
tuna; drained	1 (6½ oz) can	1 (184g) can
Cheddar cheese; grated	1 cup	250 mL
onion; chopped	2 tbsp.	25 mL
pickle; chopped	2 tbsp.	25 mL
green pepper; chopped	2 tbsp.	25 mL
mayonnaise	1 cup	250 mL
salt & pepper		to taste

1:   Blend all ingredients. Spread lightly on
     toast nibbles, as for shrimp & crab.
     This is great on buns too!
2:   Place on meat rack & heat on full power
     30-45 seconds.

CRAB & MUSHROOMS:

	IMPERIAL	METRIC
crab meat; drained	1 (4.5 oz) can	1 (127g) can
lemon juice	1 tbsp.	15 mL
cream cheese	4 oz.	125 g
egg yolk	1	1
mayonnaise	¼ cup	50 mL
prepared mustard	¼ tsp.	1 mL
sliced mushrooms; drained	1 (10 oz) can	1 (284g) can
green onions; chopped	4	4

	IMPERIAL	METRIC
stuffed olives; chopped	¼ cup	50 mL
celery; finely chopped	2 stalks	2 stalks

1: Flake crab meat & mix with lemon juice.
2: Soften cream cheese 45 seconds on power level 8 (medium-high)
3: Blend cream cheese, egg yolk, mayonnaise & mustard.
4: Add remaining ingredients & mix well.
5: Spread mixture on crackers, toast rounds or buns.
6: Place on a meat rack & heat 30-45 seconds on full power.

LORRAINE'S HOT DOG NIBBLES

	IMPERIAL	METRIC
prepared mustard	½ cup	125 mL
red currant jelly	1 cup	250 mL
wieners; chopped	1 lb.	500 g

1: Combine ingredients in a covered 1qt (1L) casserole. Heat 4-6 minutes on high.

CHEESE BITES

- So fast! So easy! And so good!

	IMPERIAL	METRIC
Cheddar cheese; grated	1 cup	250 mL
mayonnaise	½ cup	125 mL
Worcestershire sauce	¼ tsp.	1 mL
prepared mustard	1 tsp.	5 mL
green onion; chopped	1	1

1: Blend cheese, mayonnaise, Worcestershire sauce & mustard.
2: Spread mixture on crackers & top with a couple of green onion pieces. DON'T overstack the crackers, as it will just run off when melted.
3: Cook uncovered, 30-45 seconds on full power, & serve immediately.

Remember; with any nibbles that you spread on crackers or toast rounds... spread them on lightly as too much makes spillovers!

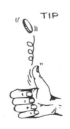

TIP

JUDY'S MEXICAN NIBBLES

-A refreshing change from nuts & bolts!

	IMPERIAL	METRIC
French-fried onions	1(3oz) can	1 (85g) can
bite-sized square corn cereal	2 cups	500 mL
shoestring potato chips	1(4oz) pkg.	1(150g) pkg.
peanuts	¾ cup	175 mL
margarine or butter	¼ cup	50 mL
taco seasoning mix	½ pkg.	½ pkg.

1: Combine onions, cereal, chips & peanuts in a 9"x13" (23 cm x 33 cm) pan.

2: Melt margarine or butter in a small cup, 45 seconds on high power.

3: Drizzle melted margarine or butter over top & stir well.

4: Sprinkle seasoning mix evenly & stir again.

5: Bake on high power, 6-8 minutes, stirring 2-3 times.

HOT MEXICAN BEAN DIP

- This is great with tortilla chips!
(Another one of Mom's recipes.)

	IMPERIAL	METRIC
pork & beans; in tomato sauce	1 (19 oz.) can	1 (540 mL) can
Cheddar cheese; shredded	½ cup	125 mL
garlic salt	1 tsp.	5 mL
chili powder	1 tsp.	5 mL
salt	½ tsp.	2 mL
cayenne pepper	⅛ tsp.	0.5 mL
vinegar	2 tsp.	10 mL
Worcestershire sauce	2 tsp.	10 mL
liquid smoke	½ tsp.	2 mL
crisp bacon; crumbled	4 slices	

1: Purée beans in a blender or food processor. Combine all ingredients except bacon. Microwave on full power 2½ - 3½ minutes, or until heated
through & cheese melts.

2: Top with crisp bacon & serve.
I love it !!

Remember:
You can cook most foods
in the microwave faster
than you can pre-heat
your conventional oven!

TIP

CRAB·STUFFED MUSHROOMS

- Wendy's special!

	IMPERIAL	METRIC
large firm mushrooms	12	
onion; finely chopped	2 tbsp.	25 mL
butter or margarine	1 tbsp.	15 mL
green onion; chopped	1 tbsp.	15 mL
cayenne	'dash'	
prepared English mustard	1 tsp.	5 mL
Bon Appetit	1 tsp.	5 mL
lemon juice	1½ tbsp.	20 mL
Worcestershire sauce	1½ tsp.	7 mL
crab meat; drained	1 (4.5oz) can	1 (127g) can
sherry	2 tbsp.	25 mL
flour	1 tbsp.	15 mL
cream	2 tbsp.	25 mL

1: Rinse mushrooms & remove stems. Thinly slice tender part of stem & combine with onion & butter in a casserole. Cook on full power 1-1½ minutes.

2: Add remaining ingredients except the mushroom caps. Cook on full power, covered for 1½-2 minutes.

3: Pile mushroom caps high with the mixture & place on meat rack. Cook on full power, uncovered, 3-4 minutes.

4: Arrange on a bed of lettuce on a serving platter, & serve immediately.

STUFFED MUSHROOMS

	IMPERIAL	METRIC
mushrooms	12	
onion; finely chopped	2 tbsp.	25 mL
butter or margarine	1 tbsp.	15 mL
soft bread crumbs	½ cup	125 mL
bacon bits	1 tbsp.	15 mL
Parmesan cheese	1 tbsp.	15 mL
salt	¼ tsp.	1 mL
parsley flakes	½ tsp.	2 mL

1: Wash mushrooms; remove stems & chop stems. Combine stems, onion, & butter in a casserole & cook on full power 1-1½ minutes.

2: Add remaining ingredients, except the mushroom caps. Mix well.

3: Stuff mushroom caps with the mixture & place on meat rack. Cook on full power, uncovered, for 3-4 minutes.

4: Arrange on a bed of lettuce on a serving platter & serve immediately.

TIP

If a microwave recipe doesn't give you a power level, you can assume it's done on full power.

MICRO NOTES

Soups

SOUP STOCK

- So fast & easy in the microwave! Don't throw away a thing!

CHICKEN STOCK:

	IMPERIAL	METRIC
chicken bones or carcass		
water; boiling	4 cups	1 L
celery; chopped	1 stalk	
onion; chopped	1 medium	
thyme	½ tsp.	2 mL
salt	1 tsp.	5 mL
pepper	½ tsp.	2 mL
chicken bouillon cubes	2	2

1: Combine all ingredients in a covered 2 qt. (2L) casserole. Microwave on full power for 20 minutes.

2: Let stand 1 hour for "carry-over cooking time".

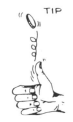

TIP

For a small family ... save chicken bones in your freezer. When you've collected enough, make a soup stock!

BEEF STOCK:

	IMPERIAL	METRIC
beef bones or		
ground beef	½ lb.	250 g
water; boiling	4 cups	I L
carrot; sliced	I medium	
onion; chopped	I medium	
bay leaves	2	2
thyme	¼ tsp.	I mL
celery; chopped	I stalk	
beef bouillon cube	I	I
salt	I tsp.	5 mL
pepper	½ tsp.	2 mL

1: Combine all ingredients in a covered 2 qt (2 L) casserole. Microwave on full power for 20 minutes.

2: Let stand I hour for "carry-over cooking time".

Freeze soup stock in ice-cube trays... GREAT for adding to soups, stews, sauces or gravy!

TIP

LOUISE'S PEA SOUP

-A family favourite my sister-in-law, Louise, makes during those "cold Winnipeg winters"!

	IMPERIAL	METRIC
ham bone	1	1
potatoes	2	2
carrots	2	2
celery leaves	a few	a few
water; boiling	3 qts.	3 L
yellow split peas	1 (16oz) pkg.	1 (450g) pkg.

1: Cook above ingredients in a large covered casserole for 20 minutes on high power.

2: Cook another 60 minutes on medium power, & then let stand for 1 hour "carry-over cooking time".

3: Take out bone, strain, & purée the cooked vegetables. Stir the puréed mixture back into the soup & serve.

TIP

Serve this with fresh home-made bread and you'll think you're in HEAVEN!

CREAM OF SPINACH SOUP

	IMPERIAL	METRIC
spinach	1 (10 oz) pkg.	1 (283 g) pkg.
flour	3 tbsp.	50 mL
onion; sliced	1 small	1 small
milk	1½ cups	375 mL
chicken stock	1 cup	250 mL
salt & pepper	to taste	to taste
green onion; chopped	1	1

1: Purée spinach, flour & onion.
2: Blend in milk & chicken stock. Purée until smooth.
3: Cook in a covered casserole on half power (medium or power level 5), for 10-12 minutes, stirring 2-3 times. Season to taste & garnish with green onion.

You can use your temperature probe for heating soups: 150° for "cream-base" soups & 160° for "water-base" soups. For accuracy, stir ½ way through the heating time.

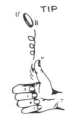
TIP

CREAMY AVOCADO SOUP

- A special treat for those special guests!

	IMPERIAL	METRIC
butter	3 tbsp.	50 mL
onion; minced	1 small	1 small
cream of chicken soup	1 (10 oz.) can	1 (284 mL) can
half & half cream	1½ cups	375 mL
milk	½ cup	125 mL
white wine	2 tbsp.	25 mL
seasoned salt	½ tsp.	2 mL
curry powder	¼ tsp.	1 mL
avocado; chopped	1	1
pepper	to taste	to taste
garlic powder	¼ tsp.	1 mL

1: Combine butter & onion. Heat on full
    power for 2½ - 3 minutes, until tender.

2: Blend in remaining ingredients &
    heat on full power for 4-6 minutes,
    until heated throughout, stirring
    once or twice. Adjust seasonings.

DIANE'S CUCUMBER SOUP

-A cold soup from one of our customers.
Thanks Dianne !!

	IMPERIAL	METRIC
cucumbers	2 medium	2 medium
onions ; sliced	¼ cup	50 mL
salt	¼ tsp.	1 mL
white pepper	¼ tsp.	1 mL
water	2 cups	500 mL
flour	¼ cup	50 mL
chicken Bovril (or bouillon)	¼ cup	50 mL
bay leaf or	1	1
garlic powder	⅛ tsp.	0.5 mL
sour cream (or plain yogurt)	¾ cup	175 mL
dill	1 tbsp.	15 mL
or chives	1 tbsp.	15 mL
or grated lemon rind	1 tbsp.	15 mL

1: Peel, seed & chop cucumbers. Combine
with onions, salt & pepper. Cook on full
power, covered, for 12-14 minutes, until cucumbers are soft. Purée until
smooth.

2: Add water, flour, stock, bay leaf or
garlic. Cook on full power for 3-5 minutes. Strain & chill.

3: Add remaining ingredients & serve
chilled. (If you're not into cold soup,
this is just as good hot !!) ☺

CREAM OF CORN SOUP

	IMPERIAL	METRIC
green pepper ; chopped	⅓ cup	75 mL
onion ; chopped	¼ cup	50 mL
butter or margarine	2 tbsp.	25 mL
cream cheese	1 (8 oz.) pkg.	1 (250g) pkg.
milk	1 cup	250 mL
chicken bouillon	1 cube	1 cube
water ; boiling	1 cup	250 mL
cream-style corn	1 (14 oz.) can	1 (398 mL) can
salt	½ tsp.	2 mL
pepper	¼ tsp.	1 mL

1: Cook onion & green pepper in butter, in a covered casserole, on full power for 3-4 minutes.

2: Stir in cream cheese. Soften on power level 5 (½ power or medium) for 1-1½ minutes. Add milk & stir until smooth.

3: Dissolve bouillon cube in boiling water; 2-3 minutes on full power for 1 cup (250 mL) Stir into cheese mixture.

4: Stir in corn, salt & pepper. Heat on full power for 2-4 minutes or until heated through.

Mmm .... mm!

BROCCOLI SOUP

- A great way to use up those broccoli stems!

	IMPERIAL	METRIC
butter or margarine	3 tbsp.	50 mL
onion; chopped	1 med.	1 med.
chicken stock or bouillon or Bovril	4 cups	1 L
broccoli ; stems peeled	1½ lbs.	750 g
milk	½ cup	125 mL
egg yolk	1	1
salt	½ tsp.	2 mL
pepper	⅛ tsp.	0.5 mL
fresh parsley or green onion; chopped	¼ cup	50 mL

1: Combine butter & onion in a covered casserole & cook on full power for 3-5 minutes.

2: Add chicken stock & chopped broccoli. Cook, covered, on full power for 15-20 minutes.

3: Beat milk & egg together, add to the mixture, & cook another 2 minutes. Let stand another 3-5 minutes.

4: Purée soup, add salt & pepper to taste & garnish with parsley or green onion.

	IMPERIAL	METRIC
cream of mushroom soup	1 (10 oz.) can	1 (284 mL) can
cream of asparagus soup	1 (10 oz.) can	1 (284 mL) can
milk or cereal cream	see step #1 below	
parsley	garnish	garnish

1: Empty both soup cans into a batter bowl. Top up each empty can with milk or cream & add to the soups. Mix.
2: Heat mixture on full power for 7-9 minutes, or set temperature probe to 150°.
3: Garnish with parsley & serve.

TOMATO BEEF SOUP

- Sometimes you can get a really nice soup by blending other soups. Try this one.

	IMPERIAL	METRIC
consommé soup	1 (10 oz.) can	1 (284 mL) can
tomato bisque soup	1 (10 oz.) can	1 (284 mL) can
water	1½ cans	426 mL

1: Mix & heat on full power for 7-9 minutes, or set temperature probe to 160°.
2: Garnish with sour cream & serve.

SEAFOOD CHOWDER

- Quick & easy !

	IMPERIAL	METRIC
onion; chopped	¼ cup	50 mL
butter or margarine	2 tbsp.	25 mL
cream of celery OR	2 (10oz) cans	2 (284 mL) cans
cream of mushroom soup		
cereal cream	see step # 2 below	
Shrimp ; drained (OR tuna OR crab)	4-6.5oz can	113-184g can
parsley	2 tbsp.	25 mL
pepper	½ tsp.	2 mL
paprika	garnish	garnish

1: Cook onion & butter in a covered casserole for 2-3 minutes, on full power.
2: Blend in soup, the 2 empty cans topped with cream, seafood, parsley & pepper. Heat on full power for 7-9 minutes or set temperature probe to 150°.
3: Garnish with paprika & serve.

LITA'S MUSHROOM SOUP

-Lita first made this for our neighbourhood dinner club ... We love it & you will too!

	IMPERIAL	METRIC
fresh mushrooms	½ lb.	250 g
butter	2 tbsp.	25 mL
salt & pepper	to taste	
flour	2 tbsp.	25 mL
soup stock OR	5 cups	1.2 L
bouillon cubes & water		
whipping cream	⅓ cup	75 mL
lemon juice	½ tsp.	2 mL
Madeira or sherry	2 tbsp.	25 mL
onion, grated	1 tsp.	5 mL

1: Wash & slice mushrooms. Combine mushrooms & butter in a covered casserole. Cook on full power 2-4 minutes or until soft. Drain off liquid & reserve with stock.

2: Season mushrooms with salt & pepper, then sprinkle with flour. Add soup stock & reserved mushroom juice. Cook on full power in a covered casserole for 10-15 minutes. (If soup looks like it will boil over in this time, turn the power level down to 7 or 8; or medium-high.)

3: Add cream, lemon juice, wine & onion. Adjust seasoning...... ENJOY!!

PREPARED SOUP MIXES:

These need time to rehydrate, and therefore take almost as long as the conventional method.

1: Prepare soup according to package directions.

2: Cook covered, on full power for 3-4 minutes.

3: Let stand covered, for 5 minutes of "carry-over cooking time."

HEATING CANNED SOUPS:

1 bowl   2-2½ minutes on full power

4 bowls   6-7 minutes on full power

OR

Set temperature probe to 160° for soups with water & 150° for soups with milk.

MICRO NOTES

Main Dishes

Cooking pasta in the microwave will take just as long as doing it the conventional method - BUT- you are saving energy with the microwave, "boil-overs" are so much easier to clean up, & many people prefer the texture of microwave pasta.

Follow the directions on the package for water & cooking times. You will find it faster to boil the water in your electric kettle. Cook pasta in a covered casserole on full power. Allow a 5 minute "carry-over cooking time" when it comes out of the oven.

TIP

Dry bread crumbs or make your own croutons ... place 1qt (1L) of crumbs or cubes in a shallow baking dish. Season if desired. Cook uncovered, 6-8 minutes on full power, stirring 2 or 3 times.

WILD RICE & BROCCOLI

- Serves 4-6

	IMPERIAL	METRIC
Uncle Ben's wild rice	1 (19 oz) pkg.	1 (540 g) pkg.
broccoli	2 heads	2 heads
mushroom soup	2 (10 oz.) cans	2 (284 mL) cans
Cheddar cheese; grated	1 cup	250 mL

1: Cook rice (with amount of water as per pkg. directions) for 15-18 min-utes on full power, in a covered cas-serole.

2: Cook broccoli in a covered casserole for 6-10 minutes on full power (* No need to add water if it's been fresh-ly washed or frozen.)

3: Mix soup & cheese.

4: Alternate soup & cheese mixture with broccoli & rice, in layers.

5: If desired, sprinkle top with crackers crumbs, croutons, or bread crumbs.

6: Bake on full power for 8-10 minutes.

7: For a variation, add a can of drained tuna to this & make it a meal.

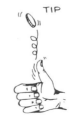
TIP

Be sure **NOT** to top casserole with cheese, or end layers with cheese... the cheese will go "rubbery" if overdone.

TUNA & RICE CASSEROLE

- Serves 4-6.

	IMPERIAL	METRIC
frozen broccoli	2 (10 oz) pkgs.	2 (283 g) pkgs.
OR fresh broccoli	1 lb.	500 g
cooked rice (see p. 150-151)	3 cups	750 mL
cream of mushroom soup,	1 (10 oz) can;	1 (284 mL) can
salt	½ tsp.	2 mL
pepper	⅛ tsp.	0.5 mL
Worcestershire sauce	1 tsp.	5 mL
tuna	2 (6.5 oz) cans;	2 (184 g) cans
Cheddar cheese; grated	2 cups	500 mL
croutons or stuffing mix	3/4 cup	175 mL

1: Cook broccoli in a covered casserole on full power for 8-9 minutes.

2: Spread rice in the bottom of an oblong casserole.

3: Combine soup, salt, pepper & Worcestershire sauce. Spoon ½ the mixture over the rice.

4: Top with tuna & cheese. Spoon remaining sauce over cheese & top with croutons or stuffing mix.

5: Cook on full power, uncovered, for 8-10 minutes. Let stand 5 minutes & serve.

COMPANY'S COMING

- A great Friday night fill in ....
- Serves 4.

	IMPERIAL	METRIC
egg noodles; or other pasta	1 cup	250 mL
butter or margarine	¼ cup	50 mL
flour	¼ cup	50 mL
milk or cream	1 cup	250 mL
chicken bouillon	1 cup	250 mL
white wine; optional	2 tbsp.	25 mL
salt	½ tsp.	2 mL
Cheddar cheese; shredded	½ cup	125 mL
green onions; chopped	¼ cup	50 mL
mushrooms; sliced	½ cup	125 mL
tuna	2 (6.5 oz) cans	2 (184 g) cans

1: Cook noodles. (see p. 48)
2: In a separate mixing bowl, combine butter, flour, milk, bouillon, wine & salt. Cook on full power for 5 minutes.
3: Stir in cheese, mushrooms, onions & tuna.
4: Combine noodles & cheese mixture in a 7" × 11" (2 L) baking dish. Cover with wax paper & cook on full power for 3-4 minutes.

see p. 48

MAIN DISHES

51

CHICKEN & RICE CASSEROLE

-A family favourite & it's so easy when it's all in one dish!   Serves 4-6.

	IMPERIAL	METRIC
long grain rice	1 cup	250 mL
mushroom soup	1 (10 oz) can	1 (184g) can
water	1½ cups	375 mL
onion; chopped	1 medium	1 medium
green pepper; chopped	1	1
parsley flakes	1 tbsp.	15 mL
garlic salt	½ tsp.	2 mL
salt & pepper	to taste	
chicken pieces	3 lbs.	1.5 kg
Parmesan cheese	¼ cup	50 mL
green onions; chopped	2	2
paprika	1 tsp.	5 mL

1: Combine rice, soup, water, onion, green pepper, parsley, garlic salt, salt & pepper in a 3 qt. (3 L) baking dish.

2: Arrange chicken over the rice. Sprinkle with cheese, green onion & paprika.

3: Cook on full power, covered with plastic wrap (turning back a corner to allow a steam vent.) Cook for 30-35 minutes. Let stand 10 minutes for "carry-over cooking time."

ZUCCHINI BAKE

-This is really tasty & a great way to use up those zucchini! Serves 4-6.

	IMPERIAL	METRIC
ground beef	1 lb.	500 g
onion ; chopped	1 medium	1 medium
celery ; chopped	½ cup	125 mL
tomato sauce	1 (8 oz) can	1 (226g) can
mushrooms ; sliced	1 cup	250 g
red wine	¼ cup	50 mL
salt	½ tsp.	2 mL
basil	½ tsp.	2 mL
pepper	¼ tsp.	1 mL
mozzarella cheese ; shredded	1 cup	250 mL
zucchini ; sliced	4 medium	4 medium
Parmesan cheese	¼ cup	50 mL

1: Combine ground beef, onion & celery in a covered casserole & cook on full power 4-6 minutes OR until meat is no longer pink. Drain if needed.

2: Mix in tomato sauce, mushrooms, wine, salt, basil & pepper

3: In an oblong baking dish, layer ⅓ of the zucchini, ⅓ of the mozzarella & ⅓ of the meat mixture. Continue in layers until all is used.

4: Sprinkle with Parmesan cheese & cover with wax paper. Cook on full power 8-10 minutes. Allow 10 min. standing time.

MACARONI & CHEESE

-This is one of my favourites!
-Serves 4-6.

	IMPERIAL	METRIC
macaroni	2 cups	500 mL
butter	2 tbsp.	25 mL
flour	2 tbsp.	25 mL
milk	2 cups	500 mL
salt	1 tsp.	5 mL
pepper	1/8 tsp.	0.5 mL
Cheddar cheese; grated	2 cups	500 mL

1: Cook macaroni per pkg. directions. (The time is no faster in the microwave, BUT- you are saving energy!) See p.48.

2: Combine butter, flour, milk, salt & pepper in a mixing bowl & cook on full power for 3-4 minutes. Stir 2-3 times to prevent lumping.

3: Stir in the cheese until melted. Mix into the macaroni.

Variation:

Stir in 1 cup (250 mL) of stewed tomatoes, which you've heated first in the microwave, for 1-1½ minutes. (You may want to drain the tomatoes before adding to the casserole.)

BRENDA'S SPAGHETTI SAUCE

- Now that's Italian!!

	IMPERIAL	METRIC
ground beef	2 lbs.	1 Kg
onion ; chopped	1 medium	1 medium
green pepper ; chopped	1	1
red pimiento	1-2	1-2
tomatoes	1 (28 oz) can	1 (840g) can
tomato bisque soup	1 (10 oz) can	1 (284 mL) can
tomato sauce (1-2 cans)	7.5 - 15 oz.	213 - 426 mL
tomato paste	1 (5½ oz) can	1 (156 mL) can
mushrooms ; (1-2 cans)	10 - 20 oz.	284 - 568 mL
salt	½ tsp.	2 mL
pepper	⅛ tsp.	0.5 mL
garlic powder	½ tsp.	2 mL
oregano	½ tsp.	2 mL
Italian seasoning	½ tsp.	2 mL

1: Cook ground beef, onion & green pepper in a covered casserole on full power for 4-6 minutes; until beef is no longer pink. Drain.

2: Add remaining ingredients. Cook, covered, on full power for 20 minutes. Let stand for at least 1 hour. (Better yet, refrigerate overnight.)

BEEF NOODLE CASSEROLE

- Friday night special!
- Serves 6.

	IMPERIAL	METRIC
ground beef	1 lb.	500 g
onion; chopped	1 medium	1 medium
cream of mushroom soup	1 (10 oz.) can	1 (284 mL) can
garlic salt	¼ tsp.	1 mL
pepper	⅛ tsp.	0.5 mL
salt	¼ tsp.	1 mL
parsley flakes	1 tbsp.	15 mL
mushroom pieces	1 cup	250 mL
uncooked noodles	4 cups	1 L
water	2½ cups	625 mL
prepared mustard	1½ tsp.	7 mL
sour cream	½ cup.	125 mL

1: Combine beef & onion in a covered casserole. Cook on full power 5-6 minutes, until beef is no longer pink. Break up meat 2-3 times during cooking time. Drain.

2: Add soup, garlic, pepper, salt, parsley, mushrooms, noodles, water & mustard.

3: Cook on full power in a covered casserole 12-14 minutes, stirring 2-3 times. Let stand 5-10 minutes for "carry-over cooking time."

4: Stir in sour cream & heat another 2 minutes on full power .... ENJOY!

SAUCY BEEF BAKE

- Spicy & HOT... cut-back on Worcestershire sauce for less "zing"!   Serves 4-6.

	IMPERIAL	METRIC
macaroni	1 cup	250 mL
Corn Flakes	3 cups	750 mL
tomato sauce	2 (7½ oz.) cans	2 (210 mL) cans
eggs	2	2
onion; chopped	⅓ cup	75 mL
salt	1½ tsp.	7 mL
pepper	¼ tsp.	1 mL
sage	¼ tsp.	1 mL
chili powder	1 tsp.	5 mL
Worcestershire sauce	2 tbsp.	25 mL
parsley flakes	2 tsp.	10 mL
ground beef	2 lbs.	1 kg

1: Cook macaroni per pkg. directions. (P.48)
2: Crush Corn Flakes & combine with tomato sauce, eggs, onions & seasonings.
3: Cook ground beef on full power 6-8 minutes, until no longer pink. Break up meat 2-3 times during cooking. Drain.
4: Combine all ingredients & bake, uncovered on high, 8-10 minutes. Let stand 5 min.

TIP

I often sprinkle the top of a casserole with crushed tortilla chips, crackers or dry seasoned bread crumbs.

MILDRED'S CHICKEN DELIGHT

- Great with leftover turkey too!
- Serves 4-6.

	IMPERIAL	METRIC
broccoli; fresh or frozen	1½ lbs	700 g
chicken; cooked & cubed	2 cups	500 mL
cream of chicken soup	1 (10 oz.) can	1 (284 mL) can
mayonnaise	⅔ cup	150 mL
cream	⅓ cup	75 mL
Cheddar cheese; grated	¾ cup	175 mL
lemon juice	1 tbsp.	15 mL
curry powder	1 tsp.	5 mL
seasoned bread crumbs	¾ cup	175 mL

1: Cook broccoli in a covered casserole 7-9 minutes on full power. Place in the bottom of a 2 qt. (2L) baking dish.

2: Arrange chicken on top of broccoli.

3: Blend soup, mayonnaise, cream, cheese, lemon juice & curry powder. Pour over chicken.

4: Top with cracker or bread crumbs & cook on full power, covered with wax paper, for 8-10 minutes. Let stand for 5 minutes "carry-over cooking time."

TUNA CASSEROLE

- Serves 4-6.

	IMPERIAL	METRIC
medium noodles	2 cups	500 mL
peas	1 cup	250 mL
onions	½ cup	125 mL
butter or margarine	2 tbsp.	25 mL
cream of mushroom soup	1(10 oz.)can	1(284 mL)can
milk	½ cup	125 mL
canned tomatoes; drained	½ cup	125 mL
canned tuna; drained	2(6.5 oz)cans	2(184 mL)cans
topping		see method #5

1: Cook noodles per pkg. directions. (P.48)
2: Cook peas in a covered casserole for 4-5 minutes. (No need to add water & no need to cook canned peas!)
3: Cook onion in butter, in a casserole, on full power for 2-3 minutes.
4: Combine all ingredients in a casserole & bake on full power, uncovered, for 6-8 minutes.
5: Top with shredded cheese, croutons, or cracker crumbs. Heat for another 1-2 minutes. Let stand for 5 minutes "carry-over cooking time."

TUNA BROCCOLI BAKE

- Serves 4-6.

	IMPERIAL	METRIC
rice	2 cups	500 mL
broccoli; fresh or frozen	2-3 stalks OR	1 (10 oz.) pkg.
cream of mushroom soup	1 (10 oz.) can	1 (284 mL) can
milk	1/3 cup	75 mL
lemon juice	1 tbsp.	15 mL
canned tuna	2 (6.5 oz.) cans	2 (184 mL) cans
processed cheese; shredded	1/2 cup	125 mL
cracker crumbs; crushed	1/4 cup	50 mL

1: Cook rice in a covered casserole. (See method P. 150-151)

2: Cut up broccoli & cook in a covered casserole 6-8 minutes on full power. Set aside.

3: In a shallow baking dish, combine soup, milk, cooked rice, lemon & tuna.

4: Bake on full power, uncovered, 5-7 minutes.

5: Arrange broccoli in spoke-fashion on top of rice mixture. Sprinkle with shredded cheese & crushed cracker crumbs. Cook for another 1 1/2 - 2 minutes on full power, uncovered.

GREAT CHILI

- And .... So easy !!

	IMPERIAL	METRIC
ground beef	2 lbs	1 kg
onion; chopped	1	1
stewed tomatoes	1 (14 oz) can	1 (389 mL) can
tomato sauce	1 (14 oz.) can	1 (389 mL) can
pork & beans OR	1 (14 oz) can	1 (389 mL) can
kidney beans		
chili powder	1- 2 tbsp.	15- 25 mL
green pepper; optional	1	1
mushrooms; optional	1 cup	250 mL

1: Combine crumbled ground beef & onion in a covered 2 qt. (2L) casserole. Cook on full power 5-6 minutes, breaking down the meat 2-3 times during the cooking time. Drain.

2: Add tomatoes, sauce, beans & chili powder. Cook, covered, 10 minutes on high power.

* Use pork & beans instead of kidney beans. The kids love it !
* If using green pepper, add to step #1.
* Add fresh or canned mushrooms to step #2.
* I often use the "Italian" stewed tomatoes.

MEATLESS LASAGNE

-This makes a great meal-in-one that can be frozen or made ahead & reheated. Serves 6-8.

	IMPERIAL	METRIC
Lasagne noodles	8	8
butter or margarine	2 tbsp.	25 mL
onion; chopped	1 medium	1 medium
garlic powder	1/8 tsp.	0.5 mL
tomato sauce	1 (14 oz.) can	1 (398 mL) can
tomato paste	1 (5½ oz.) can	1 (156 mL) can
water	3/4 cup	175 mL
beef bouillon	1 tbsp.	15 mL
sugar	1 tsp.	5 mL
basil	½ tsp.	2 mL
oregano	½ tsp.	2 mL
pepper	1/8 tsp.	0.5 mL
spinach	3/4 lb.	336 g
creamed cottage cheese	2 cups	500 mL
eggs	2 medium	2 medium
mozzarella cheese; shredded	3 cups	750 mL
Parmesan cheese	1/3 cup	175 mL

1: Cook noodles per pkg. directions. (P. 48)
2: Sauté onion in butter in a covered 1½ qt (1.5L) casserole for 2½-3 minutes on full power.
3: Stir in garlic, tomato sauce, tomato paste, water, bouillon, sugar, basil, oregano & pepper. Cook covered, on full power 8-10 minutes.

4: Cook spinach in a covered 2qt. (2L) casserole, on full power 3½-4 minutes. Drain & chop.

5: Combine spinach, cottage cheese & eggs.

6: In an 8"x12" (3L) baking dish, layer half the noodles, half the sauce, all the spinach mixture, 2 cups (500mL) of the mozzarella, the remaining noodles & then the sauce. Cover with wax paper.

7: Cook for 5 minutes on full power, then 12-14 minutes on 70% power; (medium-high).

8: Sprinkle with remaining mozzarella & Parmesan cheese. Cook, uncovered on full power for another 3-4 minutes, until the cheese is melted. Let stand for 10 minutes to set the lasagne.
ENJOY!

Your foods will take about 6 minutes/lb. (13 minutes/kg) to defrost. Remember.... don't add the weight of the dish. (For seafood see P.94)

TIP

LASAGNE

-Best I've ever had !
-Serves 6-8.

	IMPERIAL	METRIC
ground beef	1 lb	500 g
onion; chopped	1	1
garlic clove; minced OR,	1	1
garlic powder	¼ tsp	1 mL
tomato paste	2 (5½ oz.) cans	2 (156 mL) cans
canned tomatoes	1 (14 oz.) can	1 (398 mL) can
salt	1 tsp.	5 mL
pepper	⅛ tsp.	0.5 mL
bay leaf	1	1
parsley	1 tbsp.	15 mL
basil	1 tsp.	5 mL
oregano	1 tsp.	5 mL
celery ; chopped	½ cup	125 mL
mushrooms ; optional	½ cup	125 mL
lasagne noodles	8 strips	8 strips
dry cottage cheese	2 cups	500 mL
mozzarella cheese, grated	2 cups	500 mL
Parmesan cheese ; grated	½ cup	125 mL

1: Combine meat, onion & garlic in a cas-
    serole & cook on full power 3-5 minutes.
    Stir 2-3 times during cooking to break
    up the meat.

2: Drain meat & add: tomato paste, toma-
    toes, salt, pepper, bay leaf, parsley,
    basil, oregano, celery & mushrooms.

LASAGNE (cont from previous page.)

Cook uncovered, on power level 8 (or medium-high) for 10 minutes & let stand.

3: Cook noodles per pkg. directions.(P. 48)
   * The noodles could be cooked well in advance.

4: In an 8"x 12" (3L) baking dish, layer 1/3 of the meat sauce , 1/2 of the cooked noodles , 1/2 of the cottage cheese, 1/2 of the mozzarella cheese & 1/3 of the Parmesan cheese. Repeat layers & top with the remaining 1/3 of the meat sauce & the Parmesan cheese.

5: Cover with wax paper & cook on power level 8 (medium-high) for 10-12 minutes. Let stand 10 minutes.
                    GREAT !!

Note:

To cook with uncooked noodles, substitute the tomato paste & tomatoes for a 28 oz. (796mL) can of tomato sauce & 3/4 c. (175mL) water. Cook for 8 minutes on high power, covered with wax paper , then on medium-low for 32-34 minutes.

TACO SALAD

- Great for pot lucks! ... DELICIOUS!
- Serves 6.

	IMPERIAL	METRIC
ground beef	1 lb.	500 g
taco seasoning mix	1 pkg.	1 (36g) pkg.
hot water	½ cup	125 mL
corn chips	1 pkg.	1 (150g) pkg.
lettuce; shredded	½ head	½ head
Cheddar cheese; shredded	1 cup	250 mL
tomato; chopped	1-2	1-2
green onion; chopped	2-3	2-3

1: Cook meat on full power in a covered 1qt (1L) casserole, for 5-6 minutes. Drain. Add seasoning mix & water. Cook on full power 5-6 minutes longer, covered. Stir & allow to stand 5 minutes.

2: The rest is EASY! Choose your favourite serving platter & arrange the corn chips in doughnut fashion. Fill the centre of the doughnut with lettuce, just overlapping the chips.

3: The salad will now take on a pyramid shape (or you could throw it all in a glass bowl !!) Place the hot meat over the lettuce, then the cheese, tomatoes & top with green onion. For variation, add sour cream, avocado, black olives or any favourite Mexican topping.

MEXICAN CASSEROLE

-Serves 4-6.

	IMPERIAL	METRIC
ground beef	1 lb.	500 g
onion ; chopped	½ cup	125 mL
Enchilada sauce	1 cup	250 mL
tomato sauce	1 (7½ oz.) can	1 (213 mL) can
pinto beans ; drained	1 (15 oz.) can	1 (425 g) can
corn chips	1 small pkg.	1 (150g) pkg
sharp Cheddar cheese ; shredded	1 cup	250 mL
sour cream	1 cup	250 mL

1: Crumble beef & onion in a covered 2qt. (2L) casserole. Cook on full power 5-6 minutes, stirring 2-3 times to break down meat as it's cooking. Drain.

2: Stir in Enchilada & tomato sauces. Cook, covered, on full power for 5-6 minutes.

3: Stir drained beans, ½ of the corn chips & ¾ cup (175 mL) of the cheese into the meat mixture. Cook, covered, on full power for 6 minutes.

4: Top with sour cream, remaining chips & cheese. Heat 30-45 seconds on full power.

CHICKEN CHOW MEIN

- Great with fried rice. See P. 156.
- Serves 4-6.

	IMPERIAL	METRIC
celery ; chopped	1 cup	250 mL
onion ; chopped	1 medium	1 medium
green pepper ; cut in strips	1	1
butter or margarine	2 tbsp.	25 mL
bean sprouts	1 lb.	500 g
mushroom pieces	½ cup	125 mL
pimiento ; chopped	2 tbsp.	25 mL
cooked chicken ; cubed	2 cups.	500 mL
water	¾ cup	175 mL
chicken bouillon	2 tsp.	10 mL
corn starch	3 tbsp.	50 mL
soy sauce	3 tbsp.	50 mL

1: Combine celery, onion, green pepper & butter in a covered 2 qt. (2 L) casserole. Cook on full power 9-10 minutes.

2: Add bean sprouts, mushrooms, pimiento & chicken. Set aside.

3: Combine water, bouillon, cornstarch & soy sauce in a mixing bowl. Cook uncovered, on full power 6-7 minutes, until mixture thickens. Stir 2-3 times to prevent lumping, while cooking.

4: Pour sauce over vegetables & heat on full power for another 3-5 minutes.

GROUND BEEF STROGANOFF

- Serves 6.

	IMPERIAL	METRIC
ground beef	2 lbs.	1 kg
onion; chopped	1 cup	250 mL
garlic salt	2 tsp.	10 mL
salt	2 tsp.	10 mL
pepper	¼ tsp.	1 mL
mushrooms; drained	1(10 oz.) can	1(284 mL) can
cream of mushroom soup	2(10 oz.) cans	2(284 mL) cans
red wine OR water	½ cup	125 mL
dill weed; optional	½ tsp.	2 mL
dry mustard	¼ tsp.	1 mL
parsley	¼ cup	50 mL
sour cream	2 cups	500 mL
egg noodles	1(12 oz.) pkg.	1(340 g) pkg.

1: Cook ground beef & onion on full power, 4-6 minutes, until beef is no longer pink. Drain.

2: Stir in garlic, salt, pepper, mushrooms, soup, wine (or water), dill weed & mustard. Cook covered on full power for 5 minutes. Let stand for 5 minutes.

3: While meat is standing, cook noodles per pkg. directions. (P. 48)

4: Stir parsley & sour cream into the meat mixture & heat, covered, on full power for 3 minutes. Serve over hot noodles.

TOMATO SPINACH CASSEROLE

- Popeye's favourite!!
- Serves 4.

	IMPERIAL	METRIC
spinach; chopped	1 (10 oz.) pkg.	1 (283 g) pkg.
ricotta cheese	¾ cup	175 mL
nutmeg	¼ tsp.	1 mL
salt	1 tsp.	5 mL
pepper	¼ tsp.	1 mL
tomatoes; thinly sliced	2	2
mozzarella cheese; grated	½ cup	125 mL
Parmesan cheese; grated	1 tbsp.	15 mL

1: Mix together spinach (thawed & drained), ricotta cheese, nutmeg, salt & pepper in a 1 qt. (1L) casserole.
2: Layer ⅓ of the spinach mixture, ⅓ of the tomatoes, & ⅓ of the mozzarella cheese. Repeat alternately until gone.
3: Top with parmesan cheese. Cover with wax paper & cook on full power for 3-5 minutes. Let stand for 5 minutes "carry-over cooking time."

TURKEY NOODLE CASSEROLE

-Great with leftovers. Substitute chicken or canned tuna for turkey. Serves 6.

	IMPERIAL	METRIC
turkey; cooked & cubed	2 cups	500 mL
onion; chopped	¼ cup	50 mL
green pepper; chopped	1 medium	1 medium
mushrooms	½ cup	125 mL
cooked macaroni	2½ cups	625 mL
milk	¼ cup	50 mL
Cheddar cheese; grated	½ cup	125 mL
Parmesan cheese	2 tbsp.	25 mL
paprika	½ tsp.	2 mL
Worcestershire sauce	½ tsp.	2 mL
dry mustard	¼ tsp.	1 mL
salt	1 tsp.	5 mL
pepper	¼ tsp.	1 mL

1: Combine all ingredients in a covered 3 qt. (3 L) casserole.
2: Cook on full power 3-4 minutes until heated through.

Remember ... the colder food is, the longer it will take to heat up. Always reheat cold food on medium-high or power level 6-8.

TIP

CURRIED BEEF

-Great served with white rice & a crisp salad.   Serves 4.

	IMPERIAL	METRIC
ground beef	1 lb.	500 g.
apple; finely chopped	1	1
onion; finely chopped	1	1
curry powder	2 tsp.	10 mL
cream of mushroom soup	1 (10 oz.) can	1 (284 mL) can
water	½ cup	125 mL

1: Combine beef, apple & onion in a 1qt. (1L) covered casserole. Cook on full power 4-6 minutes, or until meat is no longer pink. Drain if needed.

2: Combine curry, soup & water. Mix well & blend with the meat mixture. Cook 2-3 minutes or until heated through.

TIP

The ingredients in step #2 above, make a great sauce to serve over chicken or rice, as well!

ROUND STEAK CASSEROLE

-Serves 4.

	IMPERIAL	METRIC
round steak	2 lbs.	1 kg
onion; chopped.	¼ cup	50 mL
flour	¼ cup	50 mL
paprika	1 tbsp.	15 mL
salt	1 tsp.	5 mL
pepper	¼ tsp.	1 mL
thyme	¼ tsp.	1 mL
bay leaf	1	1
canned tomatoes	1 (19 oz.) can	1 (538 g) can

1: Combine all ingredients in a covered casserole or clay baker. (Pre-soak your clay baker... see TIP P. 77)

2: Cook on ½ power (level 5, medium, or slow cook) for 20-30 minutes. Let stand for 5-10 minutes "carry-over cooking time."

TIP

Cooking on ½ power will tenderize your red meats, but you may have to increase the cooking time.

STROGANOFF CASSEROLE

-A complete meal! Also great with left-over turkey. Serves 4.

	IMPERIAL	METRIC
cream of celery OR chicken soup	1 (10 oz.) can	1 (284 g) can
sour cream	½ cup	125 mL
milk	½ cup	125 mL
chicken, turkey or tuna	1 cup	250 mL
parsley	2 tbsp.	25 mL
pimiento; chopped	2 tbsp.	25 mL
salt	¼ tsp.	1 mL
pepper	⅛ tsp.	0.5 mL
egg noodles; cooked (P. 48)	2 cups	500 mL
cracker crumbs	2 tbsp.	25 mL

1: Blend all ingredients together except the cracker crumbs. Pour into a 1½-qt. (1.5 L) casserole.
2: Top with cracker crumbs & cook on full power, uncovered, for 6-9 minutes.

TIP

This casserole will work just as well with ground beef.

SALMON BUFFET

- Serves 4-6.

	IMPERIAL	METRIC
medium egg noodles	3½ cups	1 L
mayonnaise	¼ cup	50 mL
salmon; flaked	2(7¾ oz.)cans	2(220g)cans
peas; drained	2(14oz.)cans	2(398mL)cans
butter or margarine; melted	2 tbsp.	25 mL
salt	½ tsp.	2 mL
flour	2 tbsp.	25 mL
pepper	½ tsp.	2 mL
onion; grated	1 tsp.	5 mL
sour cream	1 cup	250 mL
cracker crumbs	½ cup	125 mL

1: Cook noodles per pkg. directions. (P. 48)
2: Mix drained noodles with mayonnaise & place in a 2qt.(2L) baking dish.
3: Flake salmon & spread over noodle base.
4: Combine peas, melted butter, salt, flour, pepper, onion & sour cream. Pour over salmon.
5: Sprinkle with cracker crumbs & cook on full power, covered with wax paper, for 6-9 minutes.

SALMON CASSEROLE

-Serves 4-6.

	IMPERIAL	METRIC
egg noodles	1(6oz.) pkg.	1(168g) pkg.
mayonnaise	¼ cup	50 mL
salmon; drained	2(7¾oz.)cans	2(220g) cans
cheese; grated	1 cup	250mL
butter or margarine	2 tbsp.	25 mL
flour	2 tbsp.	25mL
salt	½ tsp.	2 mL
pepper	½ tsp.	2 mL
onion; grated	1 tsp.	5 mL
sour cream	1 cup	250 mL
green beans OR peas	2(14 oz.)cans	2(398 mL)cans
cracker crumbs	½ cup	125 mL

1: Cook noodles per pkg. directions. (P.48)
2: Combine drained noodles & mayonnaise & place in a 3qt (3L) baking dish.
3: Flake salmon & spread over noodles.
4: Sprinkle grated cheese over salmon.
5: Melt butter & stir in flour, salt, pepper, onion, sour cream, & drained vegetables. Spread over cheese & top with cracker crumbs.
6: Cover with wax paper & cook on full power 8-10 minutes. Allow 5-10 minutes "carry-over cooking time."

BEEF STEW

- You can use your clay baker for this if you have one. (Soak it first.)

	IMPERIAL	METRIC
round steak	1 lb.	500 g
beef broth	4 cups	1 L
salt	1 tsp.	5 mL
pepper	⅛ tsp.	0.5 mL
onion ; chopped	1 medium	1 medium
carrots ; chopped	2	2
celery ; chopped	1 stalk	1 stalk
potatoes ; peeled & cubed	4 medium	4 medium
flour	¼ cup	50 mL

1: Combine broth & steak. In a covered casserole, cook for 5 minutes on full power & then for 20 minutes on ½ power.
2: Mix in remaining ingredients except the flour. Cook covered, another 20 minutes on full power.
3: Stir in flour & cook 3-4 minutes more on full power, to thicken gravy.

When using a clay baker in the microwave oven, soak it first & remember you may have to add a couple of minutes to the cooking time, due to the moisture in the clay.

TIP

SUZANNE'S RANCHERS BEEF STEW

	IMPERIAL	METRIC
pearl barley	½ cup	125 mL
beef broth	6 cups	1.5 L
ground beef	1 lb.	½ kg
salt	1 tsp.	5 mL
onion ; chopped	1 medium	1 medium
carrots; chopped	2	2
celery ; chopped	½ cup	125 mL
pepper	⅛ tsp.	0.5 mL

1: Combine barley & beef broth. Cook covered, for 20 minutes on full power. Let stand on the counter 1 hour (or do this the night before.) This allows the barley to rehydrate.

2: In a separate covered casserole, cook ground beef 4-6 minutes on full power, stirring 2-3 times to break up the meat as it's cooking. Drain.

3: Combine barley-broth mixture, cooked ground beef & remaining ingredients. Cook covered, for 20 minutes on high.

TIP :

I often throw in leftover vegetables or beef gravy towards the end of the cooking time.

RANCHERS BEEF STEW
(con't from previous page)

<u>VARIATION</u>: RANCHERS BEEF STEW

You can skip step #1 & add 4 potatoes (cubed) with the other vegetables
in step #3. Also add 5-10 minutes to
the cooking time.

Save on casseroles in the
freezer... line your favorite
dish with plastic wrap & fill
with your casserole, soup etc.
When frozen, lift "cube" out of
dish & put into a freezer bag.
The cube will fit neatly back
into the dish for defrosting
& heating, plus the dish
hasn't been "tied-up" in the
freezer!

TIP

MICRO NOTES

Barbecued Ribs page 85
Allison's Baked Potatoes page 146

Meats

ROAST OF BEEF

- For roasted potatoes with your roast beef, see "TIP" P. 138.

Place roast, fat side down, on a micro-wave meat rack. Season as desired. Avoid salt as it tends to dry out the meat. Cover with a loose tent of wax paper.

Always do roasts on ½ power (level 5 or medium). This allows the connect-ive tissue to break down & tenderizes the meat.

Allow 9-14 minutes/lb. (19½ minutes /kg) on ½ power, & allow 15 minutes "carry-over cooking time."

To reheat beef, allow 30-45 seconds per slice, covered with wax paper.

Temperature Probe Cooking:
Set your probe according to the man-ufacturer's directions.
* The tip of the probe should be in the center of the meat, away from bone, fat or air pockets. The usual settings are:
130° - Rare
150° - Medium (also soups & casseroles)
170°-180° - Well done (beef, pork, lamb)
(For Poultry see TIP on P. 107)

ROAST OF PORK OR LAMB

Follow instructions as for roast of beef on previous page.

These roasts are really nice glazed with apple, currant or mint jelly before roasting.

Allow 13 minutes / lb. (28½ minutes/ kg) on ½ power for pork & lamb well done. Allow 15 minutes "carry-over cooking time."

GRAVY

	IMPERIAL	METRIC
flour	¼ cup	50 mL
water	1½ cups	375 mL
drippings; or beef bouillon	½ cup	125 mL
salt & pepper	to taste	to taste

1: Blend flour & hot drippings first, then add remaining ingredients. Heat 3-4 minutes on full power, until thickened. You can also use beef bouillon.

STEAK

-The best way to cook steak in the micro-wave is with a browning grill.

1: Preheat the browning grill according to the directions that come with your model. (Usually 5-8 minutes.) Put ½ lb. (¼ kg) of steak on your hot grill with the back of a spatula. Flip steak over & sear other side immediately.

 - Allow 2 minutes on full power for a medium steak.
 - Allow 3 minutes on full power for a well-done steak.

2: If you don't have a browning grill, "GET ONE!!" In the meantime, place your steak on a meat rack & brush steak with Kitchen Bouquet or other browning agent. The reason a browning grill is best, is because steak cooks "too fast to brown!"

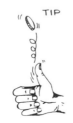 TIP

For a winter "treat", sear a supply of steaks on the barbecue & store in freezer bags in the freezer.... they'll taste just like they were barbecued! ☺ Follow step #1.

BARBECUED RIBS

- Serves 6-8.

	IMPERIAL	METRIC
country-style ribs	3-4 lbs.	1.5-2 kg
ketchup	½ cup	125 mL
garlic; minced	1 clove	1 clove
brown sugar	2 tbsp.	25 mL
Worcestershire sauce	1 tbsp.	15 mL
lemon juice	1 tbsp.	15 mL
salt	½ tsp.	2 mL
dry mustard	½ tsp.	2 mL
horseradish	½ tsp.	2 mL

1: Arrange ribs in an oblong pan. Cover with wax paper & cook on ½ power for 20-25 minutes, rearranging ½ way through cooking time. Drain.

2: Combine remaining ingredients & pour over ribs. Cook covered, on full power for 8-10 minutes. Let stand 10 minutes "carry-over cooking time."

Great done in a clay baker. Soak the clay baker as you would for conventional use. (You may have to add 1-2 minutes to the cooking time.)

TIP

STUFFED PORK CHOPS

- Serves 6.

	IMPERIAL	METRIC
thick pork chops ; with pocket	6	6
OR thin pork chops; sandwiched together		
herbed stuffing mix ; prepared	2 cups	500 mL
OR homemade poultry stuffing		
cream of mushroom soup	1(10oz.)can	1(284mL)can
kitchen Bouquet		

1: Spoon stuffing into pockets or between thin chops. Top with condensed soup thinned with a little milk OR brush with Kitchen Bouquet.

2: Place in a baking dish & cover with wax paper. Cook on ½ power (medium, level 5, or defrost - if no other settings.) for 20-25 minutes. Let stand 5-10 minutes "carry-over cooking time."

 TIP

Cover foods you wish to steam with a glass lid or plastic wrap.

Cover foods you wish to roast with wax paper or no cover.

HAM

Ready-to-eat ham ; 3 minutes /lb. (6½ minutes/kg)
fresh ham ; 8 minutes /lb. (17½ minutes/kg)

1: Place ham on a meat rack & cover
   with a loose tent of wax paper.
   Allow 10-15 minutes standing time.

ORANGE SAUCE

- One of the nicest! ... serve with ham.

	IMPERIAL	METRIC
mandarin oranges	1(11 oz.) can	1(308 mL)can
brown sugar	½ cup	125 mL
raisins	½ cup	125 mL
cornstarch	1½ tbsp.	25 mL
dry mustard	½ tsp.	2 mL
grated orange peel	1 tbsp.	15 mL
lemon juice	1 tbsp.	15 mL
butter or margarine	1 tbsp.	15 mL

1: Drain oranges into a batter bowl & add
   enough water to juice to make 1 cup
   (250mL) Add remaining ingredients.
2: Heat on full power 3½-4½ minutes. Stir
   in oranges & serve.

MEATBALLS

- Serves 4-6.

	IMPERIAL	METRIC
ground beef	1 lb.	500 g
onion; chopped OR	1 small	1 small
minced onion	1 tbsp.	15 mL
egg	1	1
salt & pepper	to taste	

1: If you want fresh onions softened in the meatballs, par cook them in a covered casserole 2-3 minutes on full power. No need to add water, but you may wish to add 1 tbsp. (15mL) of butter or margarine. This is optional.

2: Mix all ingredients together & form into 1" balls. Place on a meat rack & cook 2-3 minutes on full power, covered with wax paper. Stir & cook another 2-3 minutes if needed. Let stand for 5 minutes.

3: Serve in either of the following sauces, (next page).

TIP   If you are finding food tough ... you are overcooking! You are better off to undercook & add time if needed.

SWEET & SOUR SAUCE

-This sauce is also great with ribs!

	IMPERIAL	METRIC
ketchup	1 cup	250 mL
brown sugar	¼ cup	50 mL
water	½ cup	125 mL
onion; minced	2 tbsp.	25 mL

1:   Blend together. Add sauce to meat-balls, heat in covered casserole 3-4 minutes on full power.

LINDA'S MEATBALL SAUCE

	IMPERIAL	METRIC
white sugar	¾ cup	175 mL
vinegar	⅓ cup	75 mL
soy sauce	¼ cup	50 mL
water	⅔ cup	150 mL
cornstarch	3 tbsp.	50 mL
mushrooms, green pepper, pineapple: OPTIONAL		

1:   Mix above ingredients & heat on full power, uncovered, 2-4 minutes until thick.
2:   Add meatballs to sauce & heat, covered, 3-4 minutes on high. Let stand 5 minutes.

MEAT LOAF

- Serves 6.

	IMPERIAL	METRIC
eggs; slightly beaten	2	2
soft bread crumbs	1½ cups	375 mL
warm water	¾ cup	175 mL
onion soup mix	1 pkg.	1 pkg.
tomato sauce OR	1 (7½ oz.) can	1 (226 mL) can
ketchup	⅓ cup	75 mL
prepared mustard	2 tbsp.	25 mL
ground beef	2 lbs.	1 kg

1: Beat eggs & blend in the other ingredients.

2: Put loaf in pan, pie plate or small bundt pan. Cook, covered with wax paper, for 8-10 minutes on full power. Let stand, covered, for 5 minutes.

* Sprinkle the top with Bovril powder before baking, for a nice brown finish.

* You can also spread the following glaze on before baking:

	IMPERIAL	METRIC
brown sugar	3 tbsp.	50 mL
prepared mustard	½ tsp.	2 mL
ketchup	3 tbsp.	50 mL

SWEDISH MEATBALLS

-Serves 4-6.

	IMPERIAL	METRIC
onion; finely chopped	1 small	1 small
ground beef	1 lb.	500 g
egg	1	1
dry bread crumbs	¼ cup	50 mL
milk	2 tbsp.	25 mL
salt	½ tsp.	2 mL
pepper	⅛ tsp.	0.5 mL
cream of chicken soup	1 (10 oz.) can	1 (284 mL) can
sour cream	⅓ cup	75 mL
milk	¼ cup	50 mL
dried parsley flakes	1 tbsp.	15 mL
nutmeg	⅛ tsp.	0.5 mL

1: You may want to pre-cook the onion in a small dish for 1-2 minutes on full power; as because of the speed of cooking, they don't always cook entirely through.

2: Combine ground beef, onion, egg, crumbs, milk, salt, pepper & mix well. Form into 1" balls.

3: Arrange on a meat tray & cook, covered with wax paper, on full power 6-7 minutes. Drain.

4: Combine last 4 ingredients & pour over meat balls. Cook, covered, 5-6 minutes on full power. Let stand 5 minutes.

TAMMY'S HONEY-TERIYAKI SAUCE

-Tammy uses this on chicken, ribs, or meat.
Use your imagination ... It's great!!

	IMPERIAL	METRIC
soy sauce	½ cup	125 mL
oil	¼ cup	50 mL
dry ginger	1 tsp.	5 mL
pepper	½ tsp.	2 mL
garlic; minced	2 cloves	2 cloves
honey	½ cup	125 mL

1: Blend all ingredients together & use
as a baste for a delicious taste sen-
sation!

TIP

Hot finger towels:
Wet in lemon/water sol-
ution, wring out, fold &
roll onto a platter. Heat
30-45 seconds on full power....
What a good Hostess!!

Seafood

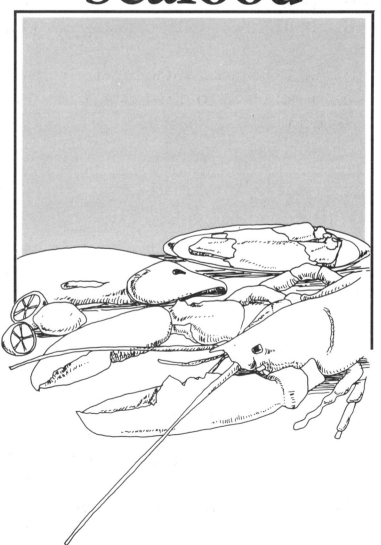

Allow 4 minutes/lb. (8.8 minutes/kg) for all your fish. It will flake with a fork when done. Don't forget that if you add stuffing or sauces, you'll have to increase your cooking time.

Cover your fish with plastic wrap for poaching, or wax paper for roasting.

For a nice steamed effect, wrap your fish in lettuce leaves.

You may also cook your fish in a brown paper bag, but make sure it's <u>not</u> recycled paper (if it is, it will be stamped on the bag.) The skin will stick to the bag as it's cooking ... when done, peel off the bag & your fish is skinned! ☺

TIP

Fish defrosts quickly in the microwave oven. Allow 4 minutes/lb. (8.8 min/kg). Don't forget your "Holding time"- P. 19

SALMON LOAF

- Serves 4-6.

	IMPERIAL	METRIC
frozen peas	1 (10 oz.) pkg.	1 (283g) pkg.
canned salmon	2 (7¾ oz.) cans	2 (220g) cans
cream of mushroom soup	1 (10 oz.) can	1 (284 mL) can
bread; cubed	3 slices	3 slices
eggs	2 medium	2 medium
onion; chopped	2 tbsp.	25 mL
salt	¼ tsp.	1 mL
dill weed	¼ tsp.	1 mL
salad dressing	2 tbsp.	25 mL
milk	2 tbsp.	25 mL
parsley	1 tsp.	5 mL

1: Cook peas in a covered casserole for 3-4 minutes on full power.

2: Combine salmon, ½ the soup, bread, eggs, onion, salt, & dill weed. Stir in peas.

3: Cook uncovered 5½-6½ minutes. Let stand 5 minutes.

4: Combine remaining soup, salad dressing, milk & parsley in a small bowl. Heat on full power 1½-2 minutes. Pour over loaf & serve.

LINDA'S FILLETS WITH HERBS

- Linda makes this in her "old" oven..... but it's great in the microwave! Serves 4.

	IMPERIAL	METRIC
fish fillets	1 lb.	500 g
paprika	1 tsp.	5 mL
parsley	1 tsp.	5 mL
pepper	¼ tsp.	1 mL
lemon juice	- a sprinkle -	
butter or margarine	1 tbsp.	15 mL
fresh lemon slices	- garnish -	
parsley	- garnish -	

1: Place fish in a baking dish. Sprinkle with paprika, parsley, pepper & lemon juice. Dot with butter.

2: Cover with wax paper & cook on full power 4-6 minutes. Let stand 5-10 minutes "carry-over cooking time." Serve with lemon slices & fresh parsley.

SOLE IN SAUCE

- So fast!   So delicious!
- Serves 6.

	IMPERIAL	METRIC
fresh mushrooms; sliced	2 cups	500 mL
green onion; chopped	2 tbsp.	25 mL
butter or margarine	1/4 cup	50 mL
sole	2 lbs.	1 kg
lemon juice	1 tbsp.	15 mL
dry white wine	1/2 cup	125 mL
flour	3 tbsp.	50 mL
cream	1/2 cup	125 mL
salt & pepper	1/2 tsp.	2 mL
fresh parsley } garnish	- few sprigs -	
lemon	1	1

1: Sauté mushrooms, onion & butter on full power, uncovered, for 2½-3½ minutes.

2: Place sole in a baking dish & top with mushroom mixture. Drizzle with lemon juice & wine.

3: Cook on full power, covered with wax paper, for 7½-8½ minutes. Let stand 5 minutes "carry-over cooking time."

4: Blend flour, cream, salt & pepper in a small bowl. Add drained liquid from fish & cook, uncovered, on full power for 2-3 minutes, stirring once or twice until mixture thickens.

5: Pour over fillets & garnish with parsley & lemon.

CRAB·STUFFED SALMON

-This makes a special meal for that special occasion.

	IMPERIAL	METRIC
onion ; chopped	½ cup	125 mL
celery ; chopped	½ cup	125 mL
butter or margarine	2 tbsp.	25 mL
dry bread crumbs	2 cups	500 mL
crab meat ; drained	1 (4.5 oz.) can	1 (127g) can
egg	1 medium	1 medium
lemon juice	2 tbsp.	25 mL
salt	½ tsp.	2 mL
salmon ; whole	3-4 lbs.	1½-2 kg

1: Cook onion, celery & butter in a covered casserole for 2-3 minutes on full power.

2: Blend in bread cubes, crab meat, egg, lemon juice & salt.

3: Salt the fish cavity & stuff with the crab mixture. Skewer with toothpicks & lace with string to hold in stuffing.

4: Place fish on a meat rack & cover with a loose tent of wax paper. Cook on full power 12-16 minutes. Let stand 5-10 minutes "carry-over cooking time."

5: Serve with lemon wedges or :
   or cucumber sauce (P. 103)
   tartar sauce (P. 103)

LOBSTER SCALLOP

-This is a recipe Jenneth Swinamer of Winnipeg gave me. It's nice with crab meat too.

	IMPERIAL	METRIC
soft bread crumbs	1½ cups	375 mL
white sauce (P.224)	2 cups	500 mL
OR cheese soup; with equal milk	1(10oz.) can	1(284mL) can
lobster meat; or crab	1(5-6oz.) can	1(142-170g) can
asparagus, drained	1(12oz.) can	1(341mL) can
salt & pepper	- to taste -	
parsley	¼ cup	50 mL
Cheddar cheese; grated	½ cup	125 mL

1: Spread ⅓ of the bread crumbs in a baking dish.
2: To the sauce, add lobster or crab, asparagus, salt, pepper & parsley. Pour over the crumb mixture.
3: Sprinkle with remaining crumbs. Cover with wax paper & cook on full power for 5-6 minutes.
4: Sprinkle with Cheddar cheese & cook uncovered for 1-1½ minutes. Allow 5 minutes "carry-over cooking time."

TERRY'S BAKED CRAB

-Put the kids to bed, light the candles, & put on the soft music ... a delicious dinner for 2!

	IMPERIAL	METRIC
crab; whole cooked	2 (6"-8")	2 (15-20cm)
eggs	2 medium	2 medium
crushed chili peppers	½ tsp.	2 mL
OR cayenne pepper	⅛-¼ tsp.	0.5-1 mL
soda crackers; crushed	6-8	6-8
salt	to taste	to taste
butter; melted	3 tbsp.	50 mL
paprika	sprinkle	

1: Carefully remove the large outer top shell of each crab. Wash the shells carefully under running water & lay on paper towel to dry. * These outer shells later become your baking dishes!

2: Now you have the task of "cracking" your crab! Collect all crab meat from the legs & the thin-shelled mid-section of the crab. (All the rest is waste)

3: In a mixing bowl, combine crab meat, eggs, chili peppers (or cayenne), crushed crackers & salt. Mix well.

4: Spoon mixture into the 2 large shells, top with a few cracker crumbs, pour melted butter over top & sprinkle liberally with paprika.

5: Cook uncovered, 3-5 minutes on full

BAKED CRAB (con't from previous page)

power. Serve with a nice tossed salad, French bread & a bottle of chilled white wine...... Hmm Mm ...

SEAFOOD QUICHE

- Make with crab, flaked salmon, shrimp etc.

	IMPERIAL	METRIC
pie shell	9"	22 cm
eggs; beaten	2 medium	2 medium
milk	½ cup	125 mL
flour	2 tbsp.	25 mL
mayonnaise	½ cup	125 mL
flaked seafood; drained	1 (4-6 oz.) can	1 (115-170 g) can
Swiss cheese; diced	6 oz.	168 g
green onions; sliced	½ cup	125 mL

1: Bake pie shell 3-5 min. on high power, uncovered. (See p.160)
2: Beat eggs & milk together. Stir in flour until smooth, then add mayonnaise.
3: Sprinkle seafood, cheese & onion evenly in pie shell. Pour egg mixture over top.
4: Bake uncovered, 6-9 minutes on full power.

HEATHER'S FISH WITH FRUIT SAUCE

	IMPERIAL	METRIC
sole, snapper or any light fish	1 lb.	500 g
parsley	1 tbsp.	15 mL
orange	1	1
lemon	1	1
lime	1	1
butter	3-4 tbsp.	50 mL

1: Place fish in a shallow baking dish. Sprinkle with parsley. Cover with plastic wrap. (Turn a corner back to allow a steam vent). Cook on full power 4-6 minutes. Allow 5 minutes "carry-over cooking time." Fish will flake easily when done. Place on a serving dish.

2: Combine the juice of ½ a lemon, ½ a lime, & ½ an orange with the butter. Cook on full power 45 seconds - 1½ minutes. Pour over cooked fish & garnish with wedges of remaining lemon, lime & orange. Serve immediately.

TIP

you will get more juice from your fruit if you heat them in the microwave. Allow 15-25 seconds on full power.

CUCUMBER SAUCE

- Great served with any seafood ...
  especially salmon!

	IMPERIAL	METRIC
sour cream	½ cup	125 mL
mayonnaise	¼ cup	50 mL
cucumber; chopped	1 cup	250 mL
salt	½ tsp.	2 mL
parsley flakes	1 tsp.	5 mL
lemon juice	1 tsp.	5 mL

1: Combine all ingredients & spoon over cooked fish. Cook on full power, un-covered, for 1-2 minutes, or until heated through.

TARTAR SAUCE

- Cream cheese style & so-o

	IMPERIAL	METRIC
cream cheese	1 (8 oz.) pkg.	1 (226 g) pkg.
mayonnaise	⅓ cup	75 mL
milk	2 tbsp.	25 mL
relish; sweet pickle	2 tsp.	10 mL
onion; finely chopped	1 tsp.	5 mL

1: Soften cream cheese on ½ power 45 sec-1½ minutes. Mix in remaining ingred-ients. Top with parsley & serve.

MICRO NOTES

Poultry

<u>ROASTING WHOLE CHICKEN OR TURKEY</u>:
- Wash poultry & salt the cavity as usual.
- Add stuffing, if desired, & secure a crust of bread in the cavity to keep the stuffing from falling out. <u>DON'T</u> use metal skewers, but tie the bird up with butcher's twine.
- Season or glaze the outside of the bird. Diluted Kitchen Bouquet <u>or</u> butter & paprika work well for extra browning. Save salting the outside as it tends to dry it out.
- You may want to start a large turkey upside-down. Place the bird on a meat rack & cover with a loose tent of wax paper.
- Allow 6-7 minutes / lb. (13-14 minutes/kg) You must add the weight of the stuffing to the weight of the bird. i.e. if you have 1 lb. of stuffing, your 10 lb. bird becomes an 11 lb. bird!
- Half way through the cooking time, check to see if any areas are overcooking. These can be shielded with aluminum foil (P.13-14)
- After cooking, allow 10-15 minutes "carry-over cooking time." Cover with a casserole or foil to keep it hot while standing.

GIBLET GRAVY

- Delicious!

	IMPERIAL	METRIC
giblets & turkey neck		
salt		see below
water		
drippings		
flour	½ cup	125 mL

1: Combine giblets, neck, dash of salt, & enough hot water to cover turkey parts. Cover & cook on full power 10-15 minutes. Let stand 1-2 hours while turkey is cooking.

2: Remove giblets & neck from broth. (The dog or cat will love the giblets!) Combine the broth, turkey drippings, & flour. If the broth is hot, blend flour with 1-1½ cups of cold water to prevent lumping ... then add to broth. Cook on full power 6-10 minutes, or until thickened, stirring 2-3 times. Adjust seasonings if needed.

I recommend that you don't use the temperature probe for cooking poultry... it is too hard to avoid bone, fat, or air pockets & the center is the last to cook.

TIP

ROAST TURKEY

-This makes an extra-special holiday!

	IMPERIAL	METRIC
turkey	10-12 lbs.	5-6 kg
oil	1/4 cup	50 mL
salt	2 tsp.	10 mL
bay leaves; finely crushed	6	6
pepper	1 tsp.	5 mL
poultry seasoning	1 tsp.	5 mL
paprika	1 tsp.	5 mL
thyme	1 tsp.	5 mL

1: Remove giblets & neck from turkey. Make giblet gravy (P.107) Wash & dry turkey.

2: Mix oil, salt, bay leaves & spices. Brush mixture on turkey & refrigerate overnight.

3: Before roasting, rinse & pat turkey dry. Stuff with Mushroom Celery Stuffing (next page) & follow roasting directions on P.106 .

MUSHROOM CELERY STUFFING

	IMPERIAL	METRIC
mushrooms	1 lb.	500 g
celery ; finely chopped	1½ cups	375 mL
onion ; finely chopped	1 large	1 large
butter or margarine	1 cup	250 mL
bread cubes	7 cups	1¾ L
poultry seasoning	2 tsp.	10 mL
salt	1 tsp.	5 mL
pepper	½ tsp.	2 mL

1: Cook mushrooms, celery, onion & butter in a covered casserole on full power 4·5 minutes.

2: Combine remaining ingredients & stuff turkey.

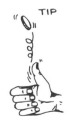
TIP

Line the cavity of your bird with cheesecloth to hold the stuffing... so easy to remove !!

CRANBERRY ORANGE SAUCE

	IMPERIAL	METRIC
cranberries; fresh or frozen	8 cups	2 L
water	2 cups	500 mL
brown sugar	1 cup	250 mL
raisins	1 cup	250 mL
oranges; peeled & diced	2	2

1: Combine cranberries & water in a covered casserole. Heat on full power 10-12 minutes.

2: Mix in sugar, raisins & oranges. Cook for 5-10 minutes longer. Cool & serve with your holiday turkey.

TIP

Don't burn your chicken on the barbecue anymore .... pre-cook it in the microwave oven first!

CORNISH GAME HENS

- Light the candles & put the kids to bed...
This is for 2 !!

	IMPERIAL	METRIC
Uncle Ben's Wild/White rice	1 (19 oz.) pkg.	1 (540 g) pkg.
Cornish game hens	2	2
onion; chopped	½ cup	125 mL
butter	2 tbsp.	25 mL
brown sugar	½ cup	125 mL
cinnamon	½ tsp.	2 mL
apricots	1 (14 oz.) can	1 (398 mL) can

1: Cook rice per pkg. directions (P. 150-151)
2: Stuff the hens with rice.
3: Cook onions & butter on full power 1-2 minutes.
4: Combine sugar, cinnamon, apricots, & their juice with the butter/onion mixture. Heat 2-3 minutes on full power.
5: Place hens on a microwave meat tray. Cover with a loose tent of wax paper & cook for <u>half</u> the cooking time. (6-7 min./lb or 13-14 min./kg). Remember to add the weight of the stuffing to the weight of the bird.
6: Pour sauce over hens & arrange apricots. Finish cooking uncovered. Let stand 5 minutes "carry-over cooking time."

CURRIED CHICKEN

- Serves 4-6.

	IMPERIAL	METRIC
apple ; finely chopped	1	1
onion ; finely chopped	1	1
butter	2 tbsp.	25 mL
curry powder	3 tsp.	15 mL
cream of mushroom soup	1 cup	250 mL
cream	1 cup	250 mL
salt	to taste	to taste
cut-up chicken	2½-3½ lbs.	1-1.5 kg
paprika	sprinkle	sprinkle

1: Sauté apple & onion in curry powder & butter for 3 minutes on full power.
2: Add soup, cream & salt.
3: Place chicken in an 8"x 12" (20 x 25 cm) baking pan.
4: Cover with sauce & sprinkle with paprika. Cover with wax paper & bake 12-14 minutes on full power.

 TIP

This is really nice served with:
Almond Rice P. 155

CAROL'S HONEY CHICKEN

- Another "conventional" recipe that is just as good in the microwave oven! Serves 4-6.

	IMPERIAL	METRIC
butter	⅓ cup	75 mL
honey	½ cup	125 mL
prepared mustard	¼ cup	50 mL
curry powder	3 tsp.	15 mL
cut-up chicken	2½-3 lb.	1-1.5 kg.

1: Combine all ingredients, except chicken, in a bowl. Cook on full power, uncovered, for 45 seconds - 1 minute, to liquify, & mix well.

2: Place chicken pieces in an 8"x 12" (20-25 cm) baking pan & pour mixture over chicken.

3: Cover with wax paper & cook on full power for 12-14 minutes.

The sauce in this recipe is also great on cooked carrots.

TIP

HERBED CHICKEN

POULTRY

114

- Serves 4-6.

	IMPERIAL	METRIC
herb stuffing mix	1 (6 oz.) pkg.	1 (170 g) pkg.
chicken pieces	3 lbs.	1.5 kg
cream of mushroom soup	1 (10 oz.) can	1 (284 mL) can
OR cream of celery soup		
OR cream of chicken soup		
pepper	1/8 tsp.	0.5 mL

1: Prepare stuffing per pkg. directions. Place stuffing in the bottom of an oblong dish.

2: Top with chicken pieces, then soup, & finally the pepper.

3: Cook, covered with wax paper, 20-25 minutes on full power. Let stand 5-10 minutes "carry-over cooking time."

TIP

A similar recipe done with pork chops can be found on P. 86

CHICKEN À LA KING

-A great way to use up that leftover chicken or turkey! Serves 4-6.

	IMPERIAL	METRIC
mushrooms; sliced	1 (6 oz.) can	1 (168 mL) can
green pepper; chopped	½ cup	125 mL
celery; chopped	½ cup	125 mL
butter or margarine	2 tbsp.	25 mL
cream of chicken soup	2 (10 oz.) cans	2 (284 mL) cans
cooked chicken; diced	2 cups	500 mL
pimiento; chopped	¼ cup	50 mL

1: Drain mushrooms & save ¼ of the liquid.

2: Cook green pepper, celery & butter in a covered casserole, 2-3 minutes, on full power.

3: Stir in soup, mushrooms, mushroom liquid, chicken & pimiento. Season to taste.

4: Cook on full power 6-8 minutes in a covered casserole. Let stand 5 minutes. Serve with egg noodles or rice.

ORIENTAL CHICKEN

- Serves 4.

	IMPERIAL	METRIC
slivered almonds	½ cup	125 mL
butter or margarine	1 tbsp.	15 mL
chicken breasts; skinned & boned	4	4
celery; sliced	4 cups	1 L
soy sauce	¾ cup	175 mL
water chestnuts	1 (10 oz.) can	1 (284 mL) can
bamboo shoots	1 (10 oz.) can	1 (284 mL) can
mushroom pieces	1 cup	250 mL
water	1 cup	250 mL
chicken bouillon	2 tsp.	10 mL
cornstarch	3 tbsp.	50 mL

1: Combine almonds & butter in a glass dish & heat, uncovered, on full power for 2½-3½ minutes until toasted.

2: Cube chicken, & add celery & soy sauce.

3: Cook uncovered on full power for 6-8 minutes.

4: Stir in chestnuts, bamboo shoots, mushrooms, water, bouillon & cornstarch. Cook, covered, for 10-12 minutes on full power until mixture thickens. Stir once or twice during cooking. Sprinkle with almonds & serve.

SAUCY CHICKEN

- Serves 4.

	IMPERIAL	METRIC
chicken breasts	4	4
broccoli ; fresh or frozen	1 (10 oz.) pkg.	1 (283g) pkg.
milk	1 cup	250 mL
chicken bouillon	2 tsp.	10 mL
bread crumbs	1 slice	1 slice
paprika	½ tsp.	2 mL
celery salt	¼ tsp.	1 mL
mushrooms	½ cup	125 mL
Parmesan cheese	2 tbsp.	25 mL

1: Place chicken breasts on a meat rack & cover with wax paper. Cook on full power 6-9 minutes.

2: Cook broccoli in a covered casserole on full power for 5-7 minutes.

3: Mix together milk, bouillon, bread, paprika & celery salt.

4: Stir in mushrooms & broccoli & pour over chicken. Sprinkle with Parmesan cheese.

5: Cover with wax paper & cook on full power 2-2½ minutes, until heated through.

CHICKEN HAWAIIAN

- One of my Mother's delicious recipes, & now it's ready for the microwave! Serves 4-6.

	IMPERIAL	METRIC
chicken pieces	2½-3 lbs.	1-1.5 kg
flour	1 cup	250 mL
pineapple chunks; drained	1 cup	250 mL
juice from pineapple	⅔ cup	150 mL
honey	¼ cup	50 mL
ground ginger	¼ tsp.	1 mL
cornstarch	1 tbsp.	15 mL
corn syrup	⅓ cup	75 mL
soy sauce	1 tbsp.	15 mL
sherry	1 tbsp.	15 mL
paprika	sprinkle	sprinkle

1: Skin chicken if desired, dredge in flour & spread in a baking pan.

2: Combine pineapple & juice, & pour over chicken. Cover with wax paper & cook on full power for 15 minutes. Re-arrange the chicken pieces.

3: Combine honey, ginger, cornstarch, corn syrup, soy sauce & sherry in a small bowl. Heat on full power 3-4 minutes to thicken. Pour over the chicken, sprinkle with paprika & cook another 3-5 minutes on full power, covered with wax paper.

MILDRED'S EASY CHICKEN

-Serves 6-8.

	IMPERIAL	METRIC
cut-up chicken	6 lbs.	3 kg
kraft French dressing	1 cup	250 mL
apricot jam	1 cup	250 mL
Lipton onion soup mix	1 pkg.	1 pkg.
water	½ cup	125 mL

1: Spread chicken in a shallow baking dish. (Skin if desired... that's where the calories are!!)

2: Mix dressing, jam, soup mix & water. Heat mixture until jam dissolves (1½-2½ minutes on full power.) Pour sauce over chicken & marinate chicken in sauce for several hours or overnight.

3: Cover with wax paper & cook on full power 35-45 minutes. Let stand 10 minutes "carry-over cooking time."

CORN FLAKE-COATED CHICKEN

	IMPERIAL	METRIC
chicken pieces	1 lb.	500 g
butter or margarine ; melted	½ cup	125 mL
Corn Flakes ; crushed	2 cups	500 mL
paprika	see step 2	

1: Skin chicken, if desired, & dip into melted butter. Roll in Corn Flake crumbs until evenly coated.

2: Arrange on a meat tray. Sprinkle with plenty of paprika & a dash of pepper. Cover with paper towel.

3: Cook 6-8 minutes on full power. Let stand 5-10 minutes "carry-over cooking time."

TIP

For "Shake 'n Bake chicken"; substitute Shake 'n Bake for Corn Flakes & cook as above.

PARMESAN CHICKEN

	IMPERIAL	METRIC
dry bread crumbs	2 tbsp.	25 mL
grated Parmesan cheese	2 tbsp.	25 mL
oregano	⅛ tsp.	0.5 mL
paprika	⅛ tsp.	0.5 mL
pepper	⅛ tsp.	0.5 mL
chicken pieces	1 lb.	500 g

1: Combine crumbs, cheese, oregano, paprika & pepper in a small bowl.

2: Dip chicken into mixture, turning to coat evenly.

3: Arrange on a meat tray & cover with paper towel.

4: Cook 6-8 minutes on full power. Let stand 5-10 minutes "carry-over cooking time."

MICRO NOTES

Vegetables

- You will find a kitchen scale INVALUABLE with your vegetables!!

Allow 6 minutes/lb. (13 minutes/kg) on full power, and a 5-10 minute "carry-over cooking time" for your fresh or frozen vegetables. You will find this may vary slightly depending on whether you like your vegetables really crisp or soft.

ROOT VEGETABLES:

All vegetables that grow underground - potatoes, carrots, turnips etc. - need a little moisture to soften them up. Just barely cover the bottom of your casserole with water and cook covered.

ABOVE-GROUND VEGETABLES:

Corn, broccoli, peas, cauliflower etc. don't need any water other than the water they've been washed in, as long as they're cooked covered.

There are a couple of exceptions to the above mentioned rule. Brussel sprouts & beans from the garden seem to need extra moisture while cooking, so treat them as root vegetables.

CANNED VEGETABLES:

These really just need heating, so drain & allow 1-2 minutes /cup on full power.

BLANCHING VEGETABLES:

No more pots of boiling water in a hot kitchen!! Grab an iced tea & relax - it's a piece of cake! Prepare vegetables as for cooking (previous page). Allow 3 minutes/lb. or 6½ minutes / kg, on full power. Plunge into ice water, drain, then into freezer bags & VOILA`!

BAKED POTATO, SQUASH OR SWEET POTATO:

Wash, pierce as for conventional cooking, & allow 6 minutes / lb. (13 minutes /kg) on full power. A medium potato will take 4-6 min. on full power & 5 minutes standing time.

CORN ON THE COB:

Cook in the husk or in an oblong pan covered with plastic wrap & turning back 1 corner to allow a steam vent. Allow about 2-3 minutes/cob on full power.

VEGETABLE CASSEROLE

-Serves 4-6.

	IMPERIAL	METRIC
cooked vegetables	2 cups	500 mL
(one or any combination)		
white sauce	1 cup	250 mL
dry mustard	½ tsp.	2 mL
cheese ; shredded	1 cup	250 mL
dry bread or cracker crumbs	½ cup	125 mL

1: White sauce:

	IMPERIAL	METRIC
flour	2 tbsp.	25 mL
milk	1 cup	250 mL
butter or margarine	1 tbsp.	15 mL
salt & pepper	to taste	to taste

Mix all ingredients in a small bowl & heat on full power, uncovered, 2-4 minutes. Stir 2-3 times, otherwise the flour will settle to the bottom & lump.

2: Combine vegetables, sauce, mustard & cheese in a casserole. Sprinkle with crumbs & heat on full power, covered with wax paper, for 3-5 minutes. Let stand for 5 minutes.

CARIE'S PARTY BROCCOLI

- Delicious!!
- Serves 4-6.

	IMPERIAL	METRIC
fresh broccoli	2 lbs.	1 kg
onion	¼ cup	50 mL
butter	2 tbsp.	25 mL
sour cream	1½ cups	375 mL
sugar	2 tsp.	10 mL
poppy seeds	½ tsp.	2 mL
paprika	½ tsp.	2 mL
salt	¼ tsp.	1 mL
cayenne pepper	dash	dash
white vinegar	1 tsp.	5 mL
cashews ; chopped	½ cup	125 mL

1: Cook broccoli until tender, about 10-12 minutes. No need to add water, just wash & cook covered.

2: Sauté onion & butter in a small dish on full power for 2½-3 minutes.

3: Stir in sour cream, sugar, poppy seeds, paprika, salt, cayenne pepper & vinegar. Heat on full power for 1-2 minutes. Pour over broccoli & sprinkle with cashews.

PARSLIED POTATOES

-Serves 4-6.

	IMPERIAL	METRIC
potatoes	6 medium	6 medium
salt	1 tsp.	5 mL
water	½ cup	125 mL
butter or margarine	¼ cup	50 mL
parsley	2 tbsp.	25 mL

1: Peel potatoes, if desired, & chop to desired size. Combine potatoes, salt & water in a casserole & cook covered on full power for 12-15 minutes. Let stand 10 minutes & then drain.

2: Melt butter 30-45 seconds on full power. Pour over potatoes & sprinkle with parsley.

CARROTS WITH ORANGE SAUCE

	IMPERIAL	METRIC
cooked carrots		
orange marmalade	½ cup	125 mL
lemon juice	2 tbsp.	25 mL
butter	2 tbsp.	25 mL

1: To cooked carrots, add remaining ingredients & heat 1-2 min. on high.

MANDARIN CARROTS

- A refreshing change!
- Serves 4-6.

	IMPERIAL	METRIC
carrots; sliced	4 cups	1 L
butter	2 tbsp.	25 mL
mandarin oranges; drained	1 (10 oz.) can	1 (284 mL) can
salt	½ tsp.	2 mL
ginger	⅛ tsp.	0.5 mL

1: Place carrots in enough water to cover bottom of casserole. Cook, covered, on full power for 8-10 minutes, stirring once. Let stand 5-10 minutes "carry-over cooking time."

2: Drain carrots if necessary. Add butter, mandarin oranges, salt & ginger. Heat on full power 2 minutes just before serving.

"Withered" carrots are overcooked! ... remember the importance of "carry-over cooking time."

TIP

WILTED SPINACH

-Serves 4-6.

	IMPERIAL	METRIC
spinach	1 lb.	500 g
green onions ; chopped	6	6
radishes; sliced	6	6
hard-boiled eggs; sliced	2	2
bacon	2 slices	2 slices
sugar	1½ tbsp.	25 mL
vinegar	3 tbsp.	50 mL
water	1 tbsp.	15 mL
salt	⅛ tsp.	0.5 mL
pepper	to taste	to taste

1: Break spinach into bite-sized pieces, & add onions & radishes. Refrigerate.

2: Cook eggs, conventionally OR break into muffin cups. Gently puncture the yolk 3 or 4 times with a toothpick. Cover with plastic wrap & bake on ½ power (medium or slow cook) for 1½-2½ minutes. Allow them to finish cooking on the counter 2-3 minutes "carry-over cooking time."

3: Cook bacon on a meat rack, covered with paper towel, for 3-4 minutes on full power. Save drippings.

4: Combine drippings, sugar, vinegar, water, salt & pepper. Cook on full power, uncovered, 45 seconds - 1 minute. Pour over spinach & toss. Top with sliced eggs & crumbled bacon.

CREAMY ASPARAGUS

- Serves 4-6.

	IMPERIAL	METRIC
cut asparagus; fresh or frozen	2 (10 oz.) pkgs.	2 (283 mL) pkgs.
salad dressing	1/3 cup	75 mL
parsley flakes	1 tsp.	5 mL
onion salt	1/2 tsp.	2 mL
prepared mustard	1/2 tsp.	2 mL

1: Cook asparagus, covered, on full power for 10-12 minutes. Drain.
2: Combine salad dressing, parsley flakes, onion salt & mustard. Add to the asparagus.
3: Heat, uncovered, 1-2 minutes longer.

ORANGE-GLAZED YAMS

-Serves 4-6.

	IMPERIAL	METRIC
yams	3 large	3 large
brown sugar	¼ cup	50 mL
sugar	¼ cup	50 mL
cornstarch	1 tbsp.	15 mL
salt	⅛ tsp.	0.5 mL
orange juice	1 cup	250 mL
orange peel; grated	1 tsp.	5 mL
butter or margarine	2 tbsp.	25 mL

1: Cut yams into chunks & place in a covered casserole, with ½ cup (125 mL) of water. Cook on full power 8-10 minutes. Let stand 10 minutes. Peel.

2: Combine sugars, cornstarch, salt, juice, peel & butter. Cook on full power, uncovered, for 3-4 minutes, stirring 2-3 times to prevent lumping.

3: Pour sauce over yams. Cook on full power in a covered casserole, for 2-3 minutes. Let stand 5 minutes.

TASTY SWEET POTATOES

- A special treat served with pork.
- Serves 4-6.

	IMPERIAL	METRIC
sweet potatoes or yams	6 medium	6 medium
butter or margarine	3 tbsp.	50 mL
apple sauce	¾ cup	175 mL
cinnamon	⅛ tsp.	0.5 mL
brown sugar	2 tbsp.	25 mL

1: Bake potatoes whole, or peel & chop. Cook (in a covered casserole for chopped) on full power 12-14 minutes. Let stand for 10 minutes "carry-over cooking time."

2: Mash potatoes & mix in butter, apple-sauce & cinnamon.

3: Sprinkle with brown sugar & cook, uncovered, on full power for 4-5 minutes.

When cooking a full meal, start with whatever takes the longest to do, & then work down from there.

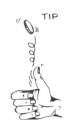
TIP

GREEN BEANS WITH TOASTED ALMONDS

-Serves 4-6.

	IMPERIAL	METRIC
butter	2 tbsp.	25 mL
slivered almonds	3 tbsp.	50 mL
French-style green beans	2 (10 oz.) pkgs.	2 (280 g) pkgs.

1: Cook butter & almonds in a casserole, uncovered, for 4-5 minutes until almonds are toasted. Stir occasionally. Remove from casserole.

2: Cook beans on full power in a covered casserole (no water needed), for 7-9 minutes. Drain, if any moisture left.

3: Stir in toasted almonds & serve.

PEA PODS & MUSHROOMS

-Serves 4-6.

	IMPERIAL	METRIC
Chinese pea pods	1 (10 oz.) pkg.	1 (283 g) pkg.
mushrooms; sliced	1 cup	250 mL

1: Combine pea pods & mushrooms in a covered casserole. Cook on full power 6-8 minutes. Allow 5 minutes "carry-over cooking time." Drain & serve.

GREEN BEANS WITH BACON

- Serves 4-6.

	IMPERIAL	METRIC
bacon	2 slices	2 slices
French-style green beans (frozen)	1 (10 oz.) pkg.	1 (283 g) pkg.

1: Cook bacon on a meat rack, covered with paper towel, for 1-1½ minutes on full power. Save drippings.
2: Cook beans, covered, for 5-7 minutes on full power (no water needed). Drain if necessary.
3: Combine bacon drippings with crumbled bacon, add to beans & serve.

PEAS & ONIONS

- Serves 4-6.

	IMPERIAL	METRIC
frozen peas	1 (10 oz.) pkg.	1 (283 g) pkg.
small onion; sliced	1	1
OR green onion; chopped	3	3
butter	2 tbsp.	25 mL

1: Combine peas, onions & butter in a covered casserole. Cook on full power 6-8 minutes. Let stand 5 minutes.

BRUSSEL SPROUTS & LEMON BUTTER

-This is a favourite!
- Serves 4-6.

	IMPERIAL	METRIC
brussel sprouts	1 lb.	½ kg
butter	2 tbsp.	25 mL
lemon juice	1½ tsp.	7 mL
salt	¼ tsp.	1 mL
Parmesan cheese	1 tbsp.	15 mL

1: Wash sprouts, trim ends & cut the base in the form of an " X". (This allows the stalk to cook more evenly.

2: Cook in a covered 1½ qt. (1.5L) casserole with ½ cup of water in the bottom. Cook for 8-10 minutes on full power. Drain. Allow 5 minutes "carry-over cooking time."

3: Melt butter on sprouts & stir in juice & salt.

4: Sprinkle with Parmesan cheese & serve.

TIP

Allow 6 minutes/lb. or 13 minutes/kg for all your vegetables. See P. 124

SCALLOPED CORN

- DELICIOUS!
- Serves 4.

	IMPERIAL	METRIC
creamed corn	1 (17 oz.) can	1 (476 mL) can
mushroom pieces; drained	½ cup	125 mL
egg	1 medium	1 medium
soda cracker crumbs	½ cup	125 mL
chives; chopped	1 tbsp.	15 mL
pepper	⅛ tsp.	0.5 mL
soda cracker crumbs	¼ cup	50 mL
butter or margarine	2 tbsp.	25 mL

1: Combine corn, mushrooms, egg, crumbs, chives & pepper in a 1 qt (1L) casserole.
2: Sprinkle with ¼ cup crumbs & dot with butter.
3: Cook uncovered, on full power for 8-9 minutes. Let stand 5 minutes "carry-over cooking time."

You can cook vegetables in plastic pouches - pierce to allow a steam vent. Avoid cooking vegetables in bags with print on them ....the print may transfer to the glass tray in the oven.

TIP

CRUMB-COATED POTATOES

	IMPERIAL	METRIC
butter or margarine	3 tbsp.	50 mL
Corn Flake crumbs	½ cup	125 mL
salt & pepper	to taste	to taste
potatoes; peeled	6 medium	6 medium

1: Melt butter in a small dish, 30-45 seconds on full power.

2: Season crumbs with salt & pepper & place in a separate dish.

3: Dip potatoes in butter, roll in crumbs & place in a glass pie plate or on a meat tray.

4: Cook on full power, covered with paper towel, for 16-18 minutes. Let stand 5 minutes.

TIP

For "roasted" potatoes:
Roll potatoes in the juice from the roast. Place in a glass pie plate, cover with wax paper & cook 6 min./lb. (13 min./kg) on full power while the roast is having it's "standing time."
See also "TIP" P. 145

VEGETABLES

138

RATATOUILLE

- A favourite Zucchini dish!
- Serves 4-6.

	IMPERIAL	METRIC
zucchini; sliced	3 medium	3 medium
onion; sliced	1-2 medium	1-2 medium
garlic salt	½ tsp.	2 mL
butter or margarine	2 tbsp.	25 mL
tomatoes; sliced	2 medium	2 medium
Parmesan cheese	¼ cup	50 mL
pepper	⅛ tsp.	0.5 mL

1: Combine zucchini, onion, garlic salt,
   & butter in a covered 2 qt. (2L) casserole. Cook on full power for 8-10 minutes. Let stand 5 minutes.
2: Stir in tomatoes & sprinkle with
   cheese & pepper.
3: Heat, uncovered, for 1-2 minutes.

GERMAN POTATO BAKE

- Really nice with ham!
- Serves 4-6.

	IMPERIAL	METRIC
potatoes	5 medium	5 medium
bacon	5 slices	5 slices
onion ; chopped	1 medium	1 medium
sugar	2 tbsp.	25 mL
flour	1 tbsp.	15 mL
beef bouillon	1 tsp.	5 mL
salt	1 tsp.	5 mL
pepper	1/8 tsp.	0.5 mL
vinegar	1/4 cup	50 mL
water	1/2 cup	125 mL

1: Scrub & pierce potatoes to bake on full power, 12-14 minutes. Let stand 5 minutes.

2: Arrange bacon on a meat rack & cover with a paper towel. Cook on full power 3½-4½ minutes. Save the drippings.

3: Combine onion & bacon drippings & cook, uncovered, 2-3 minutes on full power to sauté onions.

4: Blend onion, sugar, flour, bouillon, salt, pepper, vinegar & water. Cook on full power, uncovered, 3-4 minutes.

5: Cube or slice potatoes into hot mixture. Top with crumbled bacon & serve.

CHINESE-STYLE BROCCOLI

- Serves 4-6.

	IMPERIAL	METRIC
broccoli, chopped	2 stalks	2 stalks
peanut oil	2 tbsp.	25 mL
salt	¼ tsp.	1 mL
soy sauce	2 tsp.	10 mL
brown sugar	1½ tsp.	7 mL

1: Cook broccoli in a covered 1½ qt (1.5 L) casserole for 6-8 minutes on full power. (No need to add water if just washed) Let stand 5 minutes "carry-over cooking time."

2: Heat oil in a covered casserole for 2 minutes, then add broccoli, salt, soy sauce & brown sugar. Mix well & serve.

MUSTARD·GLAZED CARROTS

- Really nice with roast beef.
- Serves 4-6.

	IMPERIAL	METRIC
carrots	6	6
butter or margarine	2 tbsp.	25 mL
brown sugar	¼ cup	50 mL
salt	¼ tsp.	1 mL
prepared mustard	1 tbsp.	15 mL

1: Cook carrots in a covered 2 qt.(2L) casserole for 9-10 minutes on full power. (Just barely cover the bottom of the casserole with water for root vegetables.) Let stand 5-10 minutes.

2: Melt butter in a small cup, 30-45 seconds on full power. Stir in brown sugar, salt & mustard.

3: Pour glaze over drained carrots. Heat another 2 minutes & serve.

TIP

Never check to see if your food is done until it's had its "carry-over cooking time." This is when it finishes cooking.

BROCCOLI BAKE

- What a great way to serve broccoli!
Delicious!! Serves 4-6.

	IMPERIAL	METRIC
broccoli	2 stalks	2 stalks
cream of chicken soup	1 (10 oz.) can	1 (284 mL) can
sour cream	½ cup	125 mL
flour	1 tbsp.	15 mL
onion salt	1 tsp.	5 mL
pepper	⅛ tsp.	0.5 mL
butter or margarine	2 tbsp.	25 mL
herbed seasoned stuffing mix, OR croutons	¾ cup	175 mL

1: Wash & chop broccoli. If using the stalks, peel away any woody portions. Par-cook broccoli in a covered 2 qt (2L) casserole for 3-4 minutes on full power.

2: Combine soup, sour cream, flour, onion, salt & pepper. Mix in with broccoli.

3: Melt butter, 20-35 seconds, & mix with stuffing. Sprinkle over broccoli mix.

4: Bake on full power, uncovered, for 7-8 minutes.

TIP

DON'T throw away your leftovers - they "come right back to life" in the microwave oven!

BROCCOLI & CAULIFLOWER

-Serves 4-6.

broccoli; chopped   2 stalks
cauliflower   1 head

1: Wash & chop broccoli. Wash & core whole cauliflower.

2: Place cauliflower in the centre of a glass pie plate or a shallow baking dish. Arrange broccoli around cauliflower. Cover with plastic wrap. (Turn back a corner to allow a steam vent.)

3: Cook for 7-9 minutes on full power. Allow to stand 5-10 minutes "carry over cooking time."

4: Top with cheese sauce (P. 224)

TIP.
Cook corn on the cob right in the husk, 2-3 minutes/cob.
(check for extra ? protein ☹ first !!!)

Crab-stuffed Salmon page 98
Crumb-topped Tomatoes page 148
Wilted Spinach page 130

POTATO PARMESAN

-Serves 4.

	IMPERIAL	METRIC
Parmesan cheese	¼ cup	50 mL
flour	¼ cup	50 mL
salt	½ tsp.	2 mL
pepper	¼ tsp.	1 mL
butter or margarine	½ cup	125 mL
potatoes; cubed	4 medium	4 medium

1: In a bowl, mix well the cheese, flour salt & pepper.

2: Melt butter, in another bowl, 45 seconds - 1 minute on full power.

3: Dip potatoes in melted butter & then roll in cheese mixture. Arrange in a shallow baking dish & cover with paper towel. Cook for 10-12 minutes on full power. Let stand, covered, for 5-10 minutes "carry-over cooking time."

You can use seasoned bread crumbs, crushed croutons or onion soup mix in place of the first 3 ingredients in the above recipe.

TIP

ALLISON'S BAKED POTATOES

-A family favorite ; but watch out .....
they're <u>very</u> filling !!   Serves 4.

	IMPERIAL	METRIC
baked potatoes	4	4
bacon	2 slices	2 slices
sour cream	½ cup	125 mL
Cheddar cheese ; shredded	½ cup	125 mL
butter	¼ cup	50 mL
green onion ; chopped	2	2
salt & pepper	to taste	to taste

1:   Bake potatoes & cool.
2:   Cook bacon, between paper towels,
     for 1-1½ minutes on full power. Crumble.
3:   Combine sour cream, cheese, butter,
     onion, salt & pepper.
4:   Cut the side of each potato & scoop
     out potato, leaving skin intact.
     (You may need to leave a small
     portion of potato inside for support.)
     Mash the potato pulp & mix with the
     cheese mixture in step #3.
5:   Stuff potato / cheese mixture back
     into the potato skins & top with
     crumbled bacon.
6:   Reheat 1½-2 minutes, uncovered, on
     full power. Serve immediately.
     (Allison would have these
          EVERY day !!)

VEGETABLE PLATTER

- Try this "cooked vegie tray" ...
  you'll love it!

	IMPERIAL	METRIC
broccoli	1½ lbs.	750 g
cauliflower	½ head	½ head
zucchini	2 medium	2 medium
carrots	2-3 medium	2-3 medium
butter or margarine	3 tbsp.	50 mL
garlic salt ; optional	½ tsp.	2 mL
thyme	¼ tsp.	1 mL
tomatoes	2 medium	2 medium
Parmesan cheese	¼ cup	50 mL

1: Cut broccoli & cauliflower florets off stems & slice zucchini & carrots. Arrange on a "microwave safe" serving dish with broccoli around the outside edge, then cauliflower, then carrots & finally zucchini. Cover with plastic wrap, turning a corner back, & cook 9-11 minutes on full power.

2: Combine butter, garlic salt & thyme in a cup. Heat 45 sec.- 1 min. on full power.

3: Arrange tomato wedges over cooked vegetables. Drizzle butter mixture over everything & sprinkle with Parmesan cheese. Heat, uncovered, 1½- 2 minutes.

* For carrots less crunchy; par-cook them first, covered,(& with water) for 2-3 min.

CRUMB-TOPPED TOMATOES

-Serves 4.

	IMPERIAL	METRIC
tomatoes	4 medium	4 medium
dry bread crumbs	¼ cup	50 mL
Parmesan cheese	2 tbsp.	25 mL
garlic salt	¼ tsp.	1 mL
thyme	¼ tsp.	1 mL

1: Cut tomatoes in half.
2: Combine bread crumbs, cheese, garlic salt & thyme. Sprinkle over tomato halves. Cook uncovered, 3-4 minutes on full power.

* Be careful not to overcook these as they will start to collapse!!

TIP

Peel tomatoes easily by heating 1-1½ minutes each, on full power. Let stand 10 minutes before peeling.

PAT'S GREEN BEAN BAKE

-Pat & I started teaching cooking classes together...this delicious recipe is one of hers!

	IMPERIAL	METRIC
green beans, drained	2(14 oz.) cans	2(398 mL) cans
mushrooms	3/4 cup	175 mL
cream of mushroom soup	1(10 oz.) can	1(284 mL) can
cracker crumbs	1/2 cup	125 mL
OR canned onion rings	4-5	4-5

1: Combine beans, mushrooms & soup. Top with cracker crumbs or onion rings.

2: Cook, covered with wax paper, 6-9 minutes on full power. Let stand 5-10 minutes "carry-over cooking time."

MOCK HOLLANDAISE SAUCE

-So easy! Serve with vegetables, eggs etc

	IMPERIAL	METRIC
chicken soup	1(10 oz.) can	1(284 mL) can
mayonnaise	1/4 cup	50 mL
lemon juice	1 tbsp.	15 mL

1: Cook all ingredients uncovered, 45 sec.- 1 minute on full power, until heated through.

A.   BASIC LONG GRAIN RICE:
     ˜you can use wild rice too!

	IMPERIAL	METRIC
long-grain rice	1 cup	250 mL
water	2 cups	500 mL
salt	1 tsp.	5 mL

1:   Combine all ingredients in a covered casserole. Cook 12-15 minutes on full power. Let stand 5 minutes.

   * Remember how important "carry-over cooking time is ??! Well, your rice may not be done after 12-15 minutes BUT, it will be done after 5 minutes standing time.

   * A little more liquid can be added near the end of the cooking time, if the rice is not tender but nearly dry.

   * Always wash rice before cooking it.

B. BASIC MINUTE RICE:

	IMPERIAL	METRIC
water	1 cup	250 mL
salt	1 tsp.	5 mL
butter	2 tsp.	10 mL
minute rice	1 cup	250 mL

1: Bring water, salt & butter to a boil. (About 2-4 minutes on full power.)
2: Add rice & let stand covered, 5-7 min.

C: BASIC BROWN RICE:
- Brown rice takes a long time to cook in the microwave, just as it does conventionally!

	IMPERIAL	METRIC
brown rice	1 cup	250 mL
salt	1 tsp.	5 mL
butter or margarine	1 tbsp.	15 mL
water	3 cups	750 mL

1: Combine all ingredients in a covered casserole & cook on full power 7 min; then on power level 3 or defrost for 40-50 minutes. Let stand 10 minutes "carry-over cooking time".

RICE RING

	IMPERIAL	METRIC
cooked rice	4 cups	1 L
frozen peas	1 cup	250 mL
OR leftover vegetables; diced		
pimiento; diced	¼ cup	50 mL
butter or margarine	2 tbsp.	25 mL

1: Combine all ingredients & pack hot mixture into ring mold. Turn out onto a platter. Fill center if desired, & serve.

CHICKEN- FLAVORED RICE

	IMPERIAL	METRIC
chicken bouillon concentrate	1 tbsp.	15 mL
salt	1 tsp.	5 mL
tarragon	½ tsp.	2 mL
parsley	½ tsp.	2 mL
pepper	⅛ tsp.	0.5 mL

1: Add to basic rice & cook as directed.

DILL LEMON RICE

	IMPERIAL	METRIC
lemon peel; grated	1 tsp.	5 mL
dill weed	1 tsp.	5 mL
chives; chopped	1 tsp.	5 mL
salt	1 tsp.	5 mL
chicken bouillon concentrate	1 tbsp.	15 mL

1: Add to basic rice & cook as directed.

TOMATO CHEESE RICE

	IMPERIAL	METRIC
tomato juice	enough to replace the liquid	
OR stewed tomatoes & water		
onion; chopped	¼ cup	50 mL
Cheddar cheese; grated	2 cups	500 mL

1: Add to basic rice & cook as directed.

Dried foods like rice, pasta &
soup mixes take just as long
as conventional cooking, as
they need time to rehydrate.
BUT, "microwaving" saves energy!

TIP

TOMATO BEEF RICE

	IMPERIAL	METRIC
butter	3 tbsp.	50 mL
onion; finely chopped	1	1
beef bouillon cubes	2	2
tomato sauce (to replace part of the liquid)	1 (8 oz.) can	1 (244 mL) can
salt	½ tsp.	2 mL
pepper	to taste	to taste

1: Add to basic rice & cook as directed.

MOCK FRIED RICE

	IMPERIAL	METRIC
dry onion soup mix	½ pkg.	½ pkg.
soy sauce	2 tbsp.	25 mL
mushrooms (use liquid for part of water)	1 (10 oz.) can	1 (284 mL) can
vegetable oil	¼ cup	50 mL

1: Add to basic rice & cook as directed.

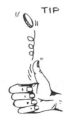 TIP

Rice freezes & reheats beautifully !! No need for more water... place in a covered casserole & allow 1-3 minutes/cup.

CONSOMMÉ RICE

	IMPERIAL	METRIC
consommé	enough to substitute water	
mushrooms	1 (10 oz.) can	1 (284 mL) can

1: Add to basic rice & cook as directed.

ALMOND RICE

	IMPERIAL	METRIC
onion	1	1
butter	¼ cup	50 mL
seedless raisins	¼ cup	50 mL
slivered almonds	¼ cup	50 mL

1: Cook rice per directions for basic rice.
2: Let stand. Sauté onion & 2 tbsp. (25 mL) of butter, on full power, in a small dish for 2½ - 3 minutes.
3: Add raisins & sautéed onions to cooked rice.
4: Combine almonds & remaining butter in a glass dish. Cook on full power, un-covered, for 4·5 minutes until almonds are lightly toasted. Add to rice mixture.

CHINESE FRIED RICE

- Really tasty! Try it with our Chicken Chow Mein on P. 68

	IMPERIAL	METRIC
long-grain rice	1 cup	250 mL
eggs	2 medium	2 medium
milk	2 tbsp.	25 mL
bacon	8 slices	8 slices
celery; chopped	½ cup	125 mL
green onion; chopped	4	4
soy sauce	⅓ cup	75 mL
garlic powder	½ tsp.	2 mL
onion powder	½ tsp.	2 mL
salt	½ tsp.	2 mL
Accent	½ tsp.	2 mL
oyster sauce; optional	2 tbsp.	25 mL

1: Cook rice as for basic rice (P. 150-151)
2: Beat eggs & milk together. Cook in a small dish for 2 minutes on full power. Cool & chop.
3: Cook bacon on a meat rack, covered with paper towel, for 6 minutes on full power.
4: Cook celery in bacon drippings for 3-4 minutes on full power.
5: Mix together: rice, eggs, crumbled bacon, celery, onions, soy sauce, garlic, onion, salt, Accent & oyster sauce. For a real treat, also add some shrimp!!

Cakes & Desserts

WARMING:

Breads are very porous & reheat very quickly. Most people overdo bread & dry it out. You'll find you can warm 1 dinner roll in 10-15 seconds & ½ dozen in 30-45 seconds. It's best if they're wrapped in paper towel, napkin, or cloth napkin. This keeps them moist but not soggy.

RISING:

If you have 10 power levels on your oven, you can rise yeast breads beautifully! Power level 1, or 10% power, is just enough to activate the yeast without killing it. Put a glass of water in the oven with the loaf of bread & microwave for 20 minutes on power level 1. (What a difference!!)

BAKING:

You can bake yeast breads in the microwave oven, but you'll find they won't crust ... & that's the best part! If you prefer the crust, you'll have to bake your bread conventionally. It will take 4-6 minutes on full power, to bake 1 loaf of bread in the microwave oven.

There are 3 very important things to know about microwaving cakes:

1: Use medium-sized <u>store bought</u> eggs instead of farm fresh or extra large eggs.

2: Let the batter sit 5-10 minutes. This step gives the leavening agent a chance to start working. Bubbles will start forming on the top & the batter will thicken up.

3: Raise the cake pan on a meat tray, inverted casserole, or microwave-safe rack while it's cooking.

Your cake is done when a toothpick comes out clean or the cake starts pulling away from the sides of the pan. If the cake still looks a little damp or glossy when it comes out of the oven <u>but</u> a tooth-pick comes out clean... then that damp-ness will evaporate in the 5-10 minutes that the cake is standing in the pan before turning it out.

PASTRY

- "NO-FAIL" PIE CRUST:

	IMPERIAL	METRIC
vinegar	1 tbsp.	15 mL
egg	1 medium	1 medium
water	5 tbsp.	75 mL
flour	2 cups	500 mL
salt	½ tsp.	2 mL
lard or shortening	1 cup	250 mL

1: Mix vinegar & egg with 5 tbsp. of water.

2: In a separate bowl, blend flour, salt & lard. Blend in as much of the vinegar mixture as needed. Always bake the bottom crust of your pie first. That will take 3-5 minutes on full power, uncovered. Then add filling & bake again according to the recipe.

3: Most microwave recipes have a streu-sel oR no topping at all. This is because pies cook too fast to brown. You'll soon adjust to this, however, there are 2 things you can do:

a) Put your microwave-baked pie under the grill on your conventional oven for a couple of minutes until brown. (DON'T use a plastic pie plate!!)

b) Brush the pie crust with egg yolk &
    vanilla <u>OR</u> with egg yolk & Worcester-
    shire sauce before baking. This will
    give you a savory pie with a nice
    golden sheen.

TARTS:

Cut tart rounds with a cookie cutter
or a drinking glass. Drape over an upside-
down muffin pan. (Make sure the muffin
pans will tolerate the heat of the pastry
ie. They should be made of polysulfone
or high heat-resistant plastic.

TIP

Ice cream taken from
the freezer can be
softened: 30-45 seconds
per pint on full power.

PECAN PIE

	IMPERIAL	METRIC
1 baked pie shell		
butter	¼ cup	50 mL
pecans ; whole or sliced	1½ cups	375 mL
dark brown sugar	1 cup	250 mL
corn syrup	½ cup	125 mL
eggs ; slightly beaten	3 medium	3 medium
vanilla	1 tsp.	5 mL

1: Melt butter in a batter bowl 30-45 seconds on full power.

2: Add pecans, sugar, syrup, eggs & vanilla. Blend well.

3: Pour into cooked pie shell & cook for 8-9 minutes on full power. Cool before serving.

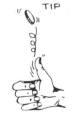

TIP

You can substitute walnuts for pecans in this recipe.

PINEAPPLE LEMON PIE

	IMPERIAL	METRIC
graham crackers; crushed	1 cup	250 mL
sugar	2 tbsp.	25 mL
butter	1/4 cup	50 mL
lemon pudding OR pie filling	1 (19 oz.) pkg.	1 (540 mL) pkg.
crushed pineapple; undrained	2 1/2 cups	625 mL
water	1/2 cup	125 mL
butter	2 tbsp.	25 mL

1: To make crumb crust, combine: cracker crumbs, sugar & butter into an 8" or 9" (1 L) glass pie plate. Heat, uncovered, for 1-1 1/2 minutes on full power. Stir & pat down into pie plate. Heat another 1 1/2-2 minutes on full power, to set crust.

2: Combine pie filling mix, undrained crushed pineapple, water & butter in a batter bowl. Cook for 7-9 minutes on full power, until boiling. Cool.

3: When filling is completely cooled, pour into crust & chill until ready to serve.

GRASSHOPPER PIE

-So easy & yet just right for that special occasion!

	IMPERIAL	METRIC
chocolate wafer crumbs	1¼ cups	300 mL
butter or margarine	¼ cup	50 mL
milk	⅔ cup	150 mL
miniature marshmallows	3 cups	750 mL
crème de menthe	¼ cup	50 mL
crème de cacao	2 tbsp.	25 mL
whipping cream, whipped	1 cup	250 mL

1: Combine crumbs & butter in an 8" or 9" (1L) glass pie plate. Heat uncovered 2-3 minutes on full power. Press into bottom & sides of pan & heat again, another 1-1½ minutes on full power. Cool.

2: Heat milk 1-2 minutes on full power until scalded.

3: Add marshmallows to milk & heat 45 seconds - 1 minute on full power, until marshmallows are melted. Chill until thickened.

4: Stir crème de menthe & crème de cacao into chilled marshmallow mixture. Fold carefully into whipped cream.

5: Pour into cooled pie crust & sprinkle top with a few crumbs of shaved chocolate. Refrigerate several hours before serving.

BANANA CREAM PIE

-Doug & I spent many special moments over a piece of Banana Cream Pie & a Coke!

	IMPERIAL	METRIC
Sugar	⅔ cup	150 mL
cornstarch	¼ cup	50 mL
salt	¼ tsp.	1 mL
milk	2¼ cups	550 mL
eggs; beaten	2 medium	2 medium
vanilla	1½ tsp.	7 mL
baked pie crust (P. 160)	1	1
OR crumb crust (P. 163)	OR -step #1 Cheescake	
bananas; sliced	2-3	2-3

1: Combine sugar, cornstarch, salt & milk. Cook uncovered, 5-6 minutes on full power, stirring 2-3 times to prevent lumping.
2: Pour a small amount of this hot mixture into the beaten eggs. Mix well & stir eggs into the hot mixture. Cook another 1-2 minutes on full power.
3: Stir in vanilla.
4: Arrange bananas in the pie crust & pour the hot mixture over top. Cool & enjoy!

LEMON MERINGUE PIE

-This is always a favorite & SO EASY in the microwave oven!

	IMPERIAL	METRIC
cornstarch	½ cup	125 mL
sugar	1⅓ cups	325 mL
boiling water	1½ cups	375 mL
egg yolks; beaten	3	3
lemon juice	½ cup	125 mL
lemon peel; grated	1 tbsp.	15 mL
butter	3 tbsp.	50 mL
baked pie crust (P.160)	1	1

1: Mix cornstarch & sugar. Stir in boiling water. Cook uncovered, 4-6 minutes on full power, stirring 2-3 times to prevent lumping.

2: Blend a little of the hot mixture with the egg yolks & then stir it all back into the mixing bowl. Cook another 30-45 seconds on full power.

3: Stir in lemon juice, peel & butter.

4: Pour into prepared crust & top with meringue... (next page)

TIP

My Dad says ... it's not what you eat that's fattening, but the quantity of it you eat that makes it fattening! I like that ...

MERINGUE

	IMPERIAL	METRIC
cornstarch	1 tbsp.	15 mL
sugar	½ cup	125 mL
water	½ cup	125 mL
egg whites	3	3

1: Combine cornstarch, sugar & water in a mixing bowl. Cook 1-1½ minutes on full power, until clear.

2: Beat egg whites until soft peaks form. Pour in cooled syrup a little at a time, beating all the while.

3: Beat at medium speed for 8 minutes.

4: Spread half of the mixture on top of the pie, sealing all of the edges. Cook 3-4 minutes on full power. (NOW- you have enough meringue to make ANOTHER pie !!)

CHEESE CAKE

-not a SINGLE calorie!!

	IMPERIAL	METRIC
graham cracker crumbs	1¼ cups	300 mL
butter or margarine	¼ cup	50 mL
cream cheese	1 (8 oz.) pkg.	1 (250g) pkg.
eggs ; beaten	2 medium	2 medium
sugar	½ cup	125 mL
salt	⅛ tsp.	0.5 mL
vanilla	1 tsp.	5 mL
almond flavoring	⅛ tsp.	0.5 mL
sour cream	1½ cups	375 mL
crushed pineapple; drained	1 (19 oz.) can	1 (540 mL) can
OR cherry pie filling		

1: Combine crumbs & butter in a pie plate or flan pan. Cook 30-45 seconds on full power to melt butter. Mix well & pat down in pan. Cook 1-1½ minutes.

2: Soften cream cheese, 45 seconds, & mix well with eggs, sugar, salt, vanilla & almond flavoring. Beat until smooth. Stir in sour cream & cook 10-12 minutes on ½ power (medium or slow cook), stirring 2 or 3 times.

3: Pour into baked crust. Cook another 2-3 minutes on ½ power, until set. Refrigerate 3-4 hours.

4: Top cold cheese cake with drained pineapple or pie filling.

CREAM CHEESE SLICE

	IMPERIAL	METRIC
graham wafer crumbs	1¾ cups	425 mL
pecans or almonds ; finely chopped	¼ cup	50 mL
cinnamon	½ tsp.	2 mL
ginger	¼ tsp.	1 mL
butter or margarine; melted	½ cup	125 mL
cream cheese ; softened	1 (8 oz.) pkg.	1 (250 g) pkg.
icing sugar ; sifted	1 cup	250 mL
Dream Whip ; whipped	1 (1½ oz.) pkg.	1 (42 g) pkg.
crushed pineapple; drained	1 (19 oz.) can	1 (540 mL) can
OR cherry pie filling		

1: Mix wafer crumbs, nuts, cinnamon, ginger & melted butter. Reserve 3 tbsp. (50 mL) for the top. Pat remaining mixture into a 9" (2.5 L) baking pan. Cook 1-1½ minutes on full power. Cool.

2: Beat together cream cheese & icing sugar. Mix in whipped Dream Whip & spread mixture on cooled crust.

3: Top with fruit topping & sprinkle remaining crumbs on top. Refrigerate.

This will also freeze very nicely!

TIP

DAVID'S VANILLA PUDDING

-So easy & there's no scorching in the microwave oven!

	IMPERIAL	METRIC
sugar	⅓ cup	175 mL
cornstarch	3 tbsp.	50 mL
salt	¼ tsp.	1 mL
milk	2 cups	500 mL
vanilla	1½ tsp.	7 mL

1: Combine all ingredients except vanilla. Cook uncovered, 5-7 minutes on full power, stirring 2-3 times to prevent lumping.
2: Stir in vanilla & serve warm.

CHOCOLATE PUDDING

1: Make vanilla pudding above.
2: Add 1 square of unsweetened chocolate (melted for 30 seconds) with the vanilla.

TIP

You can use 2 tbsp. cocoa & 1 tbsp. butter, instead of chocolate.

BUTTERSCOTCH PUDDING

	IMPERIAL	METRIC
butter or margarine	1 tbsp.	15 mL
brown sugar	½ cup	125 mL
milk	2 cups	500 mL
cornstarch	3 tbsp.	50 mL
salt	¼ tsp.	1 mL
vanilla	1 tsp.	5 mL

1: Combine butter, sugar, milk, cornstarch, & salt in a mixing bowl. Cook uncovered, 5-7 minutes on full power, stirring 2-3 times to prevent lumping.

2: Stir in vanilla & serve warm.

To scald milk, cook 1½-2 minutes on full power.

TIP

PEACH CUSTARD

- A family favorite from one of our customers & we love it too!

	IMPERIAL	METRIC
canned peaches	1 (14 oz.) can	1 (398 mL) can
eggs	3 medium	3 medium
sugar	½ cup	125 mL
nutmeg	½ tsp.	2 mL
flour	¼ cup.	50 mL
vanilla	1 tsp.	5 mL
milk	¾ cup	175 mL
butter or margarine; melted	⅓ cup	75 mL
dry white wine	½ cup	125 mL

1: Slice peaches into an 8" (1 L) glass pie plate.
2: Beat together: eggs, sugar, nutmeg, flour, vanilla, milk, melted butter & wine.
3: Pour milk mixture over peaches. Cook uncovered, 8-9 minutes on full power. Let stand 5-10 minutes "carry-over cooking time." Serve warm.

TIP

To melt butter, heat 30-45 seconds / ¼ lb. (125g) on full power.

KIM'S BAKED APPLE

- So easy & this can cook while you're eating dinner!

	IMPERIAL	METRIC
apples	as needed	as needed
brown sugar	1 tbsp/apple	15mL/apple
cinnamon	sprinkle	sprinkle
butter	1 tsp./apple	5mL/apple

1: Core apples & peel totally or just around the center. Slice or leave whole.

2: Combine sugar, cinnamon & butter. Sprinkle mixture on each apple.

3: Cook, covered, on full power as follows:

1 apple	-	2-2½ minutes
2 apples	-	3-3½ minutes
3 apples	-	4-4½ minutes
4 apples	-	5-5½ minutes

To soften butter, heat 10-15 seconds / ¼ lb. (125g) on full power.

TIP

STEWED RHUBARB

- Great with ice cream or just by itself!

	IMPERIAL	METRIC
rhubarb; sliced	4 cups	1 L
cornstarch	2 tbsp.	25 mL
orange peel; grated	1 tbsp.	15 mL
nutmeg	¼ tsp.	1 mL
sugar	1 cup	250 mL
orange juice	½ cup	125 mL

1: Combine all ingredients in a 1½ qt.(1.5L) casserole.

2: Cook covered, 8-10 minutes on full power. Let stand 5-10 minutes "carry-over cooking time."

TIP

Heat brandy for flaming desserts :
2 tbsp. - ¼ cup (25-50 mL) will take 15 seconds.

CHOCOLATE CARAMEL FONDUE

-Sharon serves this for special company!

	IMPERIAL	METRIC
caramels	1 (14oz.) pkg.	1 (425g) pkg.
water	⅓ cup	75 mL
semisweet chocolate	2 squares	2 squares
cubed fruit	4 cups	1 L
sunflower seeds	½ cup	125 mL
walnuts; chopped	½ cup	125 mL
granola	½ cup	125 mL

1: Combine caramels & 2 tbsp. (25 mL) of water in a covered casserole. Cook 2½-3½ minutes on full power, until caramels are softened. Stir in remaining water & cook another 1-1½ minutes on full power.

2: Stir in chocolate until it is melted. Cook another 1-1½ minutes if needed.

3: Serve sauce in a small fondue pot over a candle warmer. Serve seeds, nuts & granola in 3 separate dishes. Dip fruit into hot sauce & then roll in either seeds, nuts, or granola.

Your fruit can be a combination of apples, oranges, pineapple, bananas or grapes. You can also use marshmallows, cookies, pound cake or sponge candy (p.229)

TIP

OLD FASHIONED BREAD PUDDING

- If you don't like bread pudding ...
  you'll LOVE this one!

	IMPERIAL	METRIC
butter or margarine	¼ cup	50 mL
bread; cubed	4 slices	4 slices
sugar	⅔ cup	150 mL
lemon peel; grated	1 tsp.	5 mL
lemon juice	2 tbsp.	25 mL
raisins	⅓ cup	75 mL
milk	1 cup	250 mL
eggs	3 medium	3 medium
cinnamon	sprinkle	sprinkle

1: Melt butter in a 1qt (1L) casserole, 45 seconds- 1 minute on full power.

2: Add bread, sugar, lemon peel, lemon juice & raisins.

3: Combine milk & eggs. Pour over the bread mixture.

4: Sprinkle with cinnamon, then place casserole in a baking dish with 1 cup (250 mL) of warm water in it.

5: Cook uncovered, 10-12 minutes on full power.

chocolate Caramel Fondue page 175

APPLE CRISP

-The best yet! Great served with ice cream or just plain cream.

	IMPERIAL	METRIC
apples ; sliced & peeled	6	6
white sugar	1/3 cup	75 mL
flour	2 tbsp.	25 mL
cinnamon	1/2 tsp.	2 mL
butter	1 tbsp.	15 mL
lemon juice	2 tbsp.	25 mL
brown sugar ⎫	3/4 cup	175 mL
flour ⎬	3/4 cup	175 mL
butter ⎭	1/3 cup	75 mL
walnuts; chopped	1/2 cup	125 mL

1: Place apples in an 8" (20 cm) round or square pan.

2: Mix together the next 5 ingredients. Blend well with the apples.

3: Mix together the next 3 ingredients & crumble over the apple mixture. Sprinkle with chopped walnuts & then pat down with wax paper or the back of a spoon.

4: Cook uncovered, 15 minutes on full power. Put this in the oven when you're ready to sit down to dinner. No need to attend to it. Let the timer run out & it'll be ready when you are!

TIP

ELLIE'S MARS BAR SQUARE

- yummy!

	IMPERIAL	METRIC
Mars Bars ; cut up	3	3
butter or margarine	1/3 cup	75 mL
Rice krispies	3 cups	750 mL
chocolate chips	1 cup	250 mL

1: Combine Mars bars & butter in a mixing bowl. Heat uncovered, 1-1½ minutes on full power, until melted.

2: Mix in Rice krispies. Press into an 8" (20 cm) square pan.

3: Melt chocolate chips, uncovered, 45 seconds-1 minute on full power. Spread over krispie base & refrigerate until set.

RHUBARB FLUFF

-This makes a very light dessert after a heavy meal.

	IMPERIAL	METRIC
rhubarb	4 cups	1 L
sugar	¼ cup	50 mL
gelatin; plain	1 (⅓ oz.) pkg.	1 (7g) pkg
whipping cream; whipped	2 cups	½ L

1: Cook rhubarb 8-10 minutes on full power or until cooked. Stir in sugar.
2: Combine gelatin with 1 tbsp.(15 mL) of cold water & mix into rhubarb mixture. Cool.
3: Fold cooled rhubarb mixture into prepared whipping cream. Chill.

You can set bread to rise in the microwave oven.... Put a cup of water in with it & heat on 10% power (level 1) for 20 min. Anything higher will destroy the yeast.

TIP

CHOCOLATE SLICE

(NANAIMO BARS!)

	IMPERIAL	METRIC
butter or margarine	½ cup	125 mL
white sugar	2 tbsp.	25 mL
cocoa	5 tbsp.	75 mL
vanilla	1 tsp.	5 mL
egg ; beaten	1	1
graham wafer crumbs	2 cups	500 mL
coconut	1 cup	250 mL
walnuts ; chopped	½ cup	125 mL

1: Soften butter 15-30 seconds on full power. Blend in sugar, cocoa, vanilla & egg.

2: Mix in crumbs, coconut & nuts.

3: Pack into an ungreased 6"x 10" (15 x 25 cm.) pan.

4: Spread with icing as follows:

	IMPERIAL	METRIC
butter	4 tbsp.	50 mL
milk	3 tbsp.	45 mL
vanilla custard powder	2 tbsp.	30 mL
icing sugar ; sifted	2 cups	500 mL

Cream together : butter, milk & vanilla. Blend in icing sugar.

5: Top with chocolate topping as follows on next page:

	IMPERIAL	METRIC
unsweetened chocolate	4 squares	4 squares
butter	1 tbsp.	15 mL

Melt chocolate 45 seconds - 1 minute on full power. Blend in butter until smooth.

6: Spread evenly & refrigerate until set.

ANN'S GRANOLA BARS

- Great for kids' lunches!

	IMPERIAL	METRIC
butter	½ cup	125 mL
brown sugar	1 cup	250 mL
oatmeal	2 cups	500 mL
baking powder	1 tsp.	5 mL
vanilla	1 tsp.	5 mL

1: Melt butter (45 seconds) then combine with other ingredients. Press into an 8" (2L) baking pan & cook 6-8 minutes on full power. Slice when warm as it hardens as it cools.

2: See also Granola Cereal P. 235

PEANUT BUTTER SLICE

-Another of my Mother's recipes, now ready for the microwave oven. It's yummy!

	IMPERIAL	METRIC
peanut butter	I cup	250 mL
corn syrup	½ cup	125 mL
brown sugar	½ cup	125 mL
Rice Krispies	2 cups	500 mL
Corn Flakes	I cup	250 mL

1: Combine peanut butter, syrup & sugar in a mixing bowl. Heat 1-2 minutes on full power, until melted. Blend well.
2: Add cereals & mix thoroughly.
3: Place in an oblong baking pan; 7½" x 11¾" (18 x 28 cm)
4: Top with <u>caramel icing</u> as follows:

	IMPERIAL	METRIC
brown sugar	I cup	250 mL
cream; OR milk	3 tbsp.	50 mL
butter	2 tbsp.	25 mL
corn syrup	2 tbsp.	25 mL
icing sugar; sifted	¾ cup	175 mL
flour	¼ cup	50 mL

1: Boil sugar, cream, butter & syrup, full power, 4-5 minutes. (Remember -no scorching in the microwave onen!)
2: Beat in icing sugar & flour. Beat until smooth & spread on cake.

BUTTER TART SLICE

- One of Carol Jone's recipes. One of our favorites & not a SINGLE calorie!!

	IMPERIAL	METRIC
butter	½ cup	125 mL
flour	1 cup	250 mL
icing sugar	2 tbsp.	25 mL
brown sugar	1½ cups	375 mL
butter ; melted	¼ cup	50 mL
white vinegar	1 tbsp.	15 mL
eggs	2 medium	2 medium
raisins	1 cup	250 mL
vanilla	1 tsp.	5 mL

1: Mix ½ cup (125 mL) of butter with flour & icing sugar. Press into an 8" (20 cm) square pan.

2: Cook uncovered, 4·5 minutes on full power

3: Beat together the remaining ingredients, except the raisins.

4: Stir in raisins & pour over base.

5: Bake 4·6 minutes on full power.

TIP

Soften brown sugar that has become hard, by placing an open container of sugar beside 1 cup (250 mL) of water, in the oven. Heat 2-3 minutes on full power.

DEBBIE'S FAVORITE BROWNIES

	IMPERIAL	METRIC
unsweetened chocolate	2 squares	2 squares
OR .cocoa ⎱	¼ cup	50 mL
& butter ⎰	2 tbsp.	25 mL
butter	¼ cup	50 mL
sugar	1 cup	250 mL
eggs; beaten	2 medium	2 medium
flour	1 cup	250 mL
baking powder	½ tsp.	2 mL
salt	1 tsp.	5 mL
vanilla	1 tsp.	5 mL
walnuts; chopped	1 cup	250 mL

1: Melt butter & chocolate 45 seconds - 1 minute on full power.

2: Add sugar & eggs. Beat well.

3: Blend in flour, baking powder, salt & vanilla. Mix in nuts.

4: Spread into an 8"(20 cm) square or round pan. Place on a plastic meat rack & bake uncovered, 8-10 minutes on ½ power (power level 5 or medium).

5: When cooled, top with chocolate frosting.

DAVID'S MARSHMALLOW TREATS

- kids love it & it's so easy!

		IMPERIAL	METRIC
butter or margarine		¼ cup	50 mL
marshmallows	large	40	40
	OR miniature	3 cups	750 mL
vanilla		½ tsp.	2 mL
Rice krispies		5-6 cups	1.25-1.5 L

1: Melt butter & marshmallows 1½ - 2 minutes on full power. Stir in vanilla.
2: Add Rice Krispies & mix well.
3: Press into a buttered 9"x13" (23x33cm) pan. Slice when cool.

VARIATION:

Add 1 cup (250mL) of peanut butter &/or ½ cup (125 mL) of peanuts, to the melted mixture in step #1, & then complete step #2 & #3. This makes a nice snack!

MAPLE CREAM FUDGE

	IMPERIAL	METRIC
brown sugar	4 cups	1 L
flour	2 tbsp.	25 mL
baking powder	2 tsp.	10 mL
cream	1 cup	250 mL
salt	½ tsp.	2 mL
walnuts ; chopped	1 cup	250 mL

1: Combine all ingredients, except nuts, in a large casserole or mixing bowl. Cook on full power, stirring a couple of times. * Once the mixture starts to boil, it might look like it will boil over. Turn your power level down - you may need to lower it as much as to ½ power (level 5 or medium). Allow the mixture to boil until it reaches the soft ball stage (test by dropping a bit into a cup of cold water).

2: Stir in nuts, pour into an 8" (20cm) pan & refrigerate until set.

See "tips" on next page.

* Normally when a recipe calls for full power, the cooking time is in relation to that power level. If you decide you want a lower power level, to slow up the cooking time;

i.e.- tenderizing red meats , you must increase the cooking time . So a roast that would take 18 minutes on full power, will take 27 minutes on ½ power.

BUT:

If you have something at a rolling boil & you want to maintain that boil without boiling over ... you can turn down the power level. You DON'T have to increase the cooking time because it's still boiling.

(Have I confused you sufficiently !?)

WENDY'S FUDGE

- A special treat at Christmas!

	IMPERIAL	METRIC
butter	3 tbsp.	50 mL
evaporated milk; small can	⅔ cup	150 mL
white sugar	1⅓ cups	325 mL
salt	½ tsp.	2 mL
marshmallows; miniature	1½ cups	375 mL
chocolate chips	1½ cups	375 mL
maple or vanilla flavoring	½ tsp.	2 mL
chopped nuts	½ cup	125 mL

1: Combine butter, evaporated milk, sugar & salt in a batter bowl. Heat 2-4 minutes on full power, until boiling. Then boil on medium-high (power level 8) for 5 minutes.

2: Add marshmallows, chocolate, flavoring & nuts. Stir vigorously until marshmallows are melted & blended.

3: Pour into a well-greased 9" (23cm) pan. Top with cherry halves or walnuts. Cool & cut into squares.

DRENE'S SQUARES

- Easy to make & easy to freeze.

	IMPERIAL	METRIC
butterscotch Chipits	1 (12oz.) pkg.	1 (350g) pkg.
butter or margarine	½ cup	125 mL
peanut butter	1 cup	250 mL
walnuts or coconut	½ cup	125 mL
marshmallows; miniature	1 (8oz) bag	1 (250g) bag

1: Combine Chipits & butter in a batter bowl. Heat 1-1½ minutes on full power, until melted.
2: Stir in peanut butter & nuts.
3: When warm (NOT HOT), fold in marsh-mallows.
4: Place in an oblong 6"x 12" (15cm x 30cm) pan. Refrigerate & slice when cool.

JANE'S SPECIAL K SQUARES

	IMPERIAL	METRIC
peanut butter	¾ cup	175 mL
corn syrup	½ cup	125 mL
white sugar	½ cup	125 mL
Special K cereal	3 cups	750 mL
butterscotch Chipits	6 oz.	175 mL
chocolate Chipits	6 oz.	175 mL

1: Melt peanut butter, syrup & sugar in a bowl, 1-1½ minutes on full power.

2: Mix in the cereal & pat into an 8" (20 cm) square pan.

3: Melt both types of Chipits 1½-2 minutes on full power (HOW EASY!)

4: Spread topping over cereal base & allow to set in the refrigerator for 20 minutes before serving.

 TIP

Throw out the double-boiler .... with the micro-wave oven there's NO scorching!!

MATRIMONIAL CAKE

-An old favorite now ready for the microwave oven!

	IMPERIAL	METRIC
flour	1½ cups	375 mL
baking soda	½ tsp.	2 mL
baking powder	1 tsp.	5 mL
salt	¼ tsp.	1 mL
butter	1 cup	250 mL
brown sugar	1 cup	250 mL
oatmeal	1½ cups	375 mL

1: Mix all ingredients & rub together with fingers.
2: Put ½ of the mixture into a shallow 8" x 8" (2 L) pan & pat smooth.
3: Bake uncovered, 2½-3½ minutes on full power.

FILLING:

	IMPERIAL	METRIC
chopped dates	1 lb.	500 g
cold water	½ cup	125 mL
brown sugar	2 tbsp.	25 mL
orange juice	3 tbsp.	50 mL
lemon juice	2 tsp.	10 mL

1: Blend all ingredients & cook uncovered, 5-8 minutes on full power, stirring twice.
2: Spread cooled filling over crumb crust.
3: Sprinkle the other ½ of crumbs on top.
4: Bake uncovered, another 6-8 minutes on full power. Cool.

CHOCOLATE MARSHMALLOW ROLLS

	IMPERIAL	METRIC
unsweetened chocolate	2(1oz)squares	2(30g)squares
OR cocoa	3tbsp.	50 mL
+ butter	1 tbsp.	15 mL
butter	3 tbsp.	50 mL
icing sugar; sifted	1 cup	250 mL
marshmallows; miniature	1(8oz.) bag	1(250g) bag
chopped nuts	1 cup	250 mL
egg	1 medium	1 medium
coconut	see below	

1: Melt butter & chocolate uncovered, 45 seconds - 1 minute on full power.

2: Blend icing sugar, marshmallows, nuts & egg with chocolate mixture. Blend well.

3: Sprinkle 2 pieces of wax paper with approximately 1/4"(5mm) of coconut.

4: Divide chocolate-marshmallow mixture into 2, & shape each as a log.

5: Roll each log-shaped half up in coconut lined paper, shaping as you roll. Seal with aluminum foil & refrigerate before slicing.

* For a nice colourful roll, use the coloured marshmallows.

BANANA LOAF

-In a ring mold!

	IMPERIAL	METRIC
shortening ; softened	¼ cup	50 mL
sugar	½ cup	125 mL
egg ; beaten	1 medium	1 medium
bran	1 cup	250 mL
milk	2 tbsp.	25 mL
bananas ; mashed	1½ cups	375 mL
flour	1½ cups	375 mL
salt	½ tsp.	2 mL
baking powder	1 tsp.	5 mL
baking soda	½ tsp.	2 mL
vanilla	1 tsp.	5 mL
walnuts ; chopped	½ cup	125 mL

1: Blend together shortening, sugar, egg & bran.
2: Blend in milk, bananas, flour, salt, baking powder, soda & vanilla.
3: Mix in chopped walnuts.
4: Lightly grease a bundt pan & sprinkle with brown sugar or cookie crumbs. Pour batter into mold & let stand for 5 minutes <u>before</u> baking. (See P. 159)
5: Place cake pan on a meat rack. Bake uncovered, 9-11 minutes on full power. Let stand 10 minutes before inverting onto a serving plate.

REFRIGERATOR BRAN MUFFINS

-The molasses in this recipe makes a nice brown muffin.

	IMPERIAL	METRIC
All Bran cereal	3 cups	750 mL
boiling water	1 cup	250 mL
eggs; beaten	2 medium	2 medium
molasses	½ cup	125 mL
buttermilk (see footnote *)	1½ cups	375 mL
oil	½ cup	125 mL
raisins	1 cup	250 mL
baking soda	2½ tsp.	12 mL
salt	½ tsp.	2 mL
sugar	1 cup	250 mL
flour	2½ cups	625 mL

1: Pour boiling water over bran & cool.
2: Add eggs, molasses, buttermilk, oil & raisins. Blend well.
3: Stir together soda, salt, sugar & flour.
4: Stir into bran mixture. Always let batter sit for 5 minutes before baking. This batter will keep up to 5 weeks in the refrigerator!
5: Fill muffin cups ⅔ full. Bake 2-3 minutes on high power, for a tray of 6.
   * For buttermilk, you can substitute: 1½ tbsp. (50 mL) of vinegar dissolved in 1½ cups (375 mL) of milk. Let stand 5 min.

CORN MUFFINS

-The only corn muffins I can eat ...
 must be the sugar!

	IMPERIAL	METRIC
butter or margarine	¼ cup	50 mL
sugar	¼ cup	50 mL
eggs	2 medium	2 medium
buttermilk (see * p.194)	1 cup	250 mL
flour	1 cup	250 mL
cornmeal	⅔ cup	150 mL
baking powder	1 tsp.	5 mL
salt	½ tsp.	2 mL
baking soda	¼ tsp.	1 mL

1: Melt butter 30 seconds on full power.
2: Beat in sugar, eggs & buttermilk.
3: Mix in flour, cornmeal, baking powder, salt & soda. Let batter sit 5 minutes.
4: Fill muffin containers 3/4 full & bake 2½ - 3½ minutes on full power, for a tray of 6.

Plump raisins or dried fruit by adding ¾ cup (175 mL) of water to 1 cup (250 mL) of fruit, in a covered casserole or container. Cook 5 minutes on full power. Let stand 5 minutes. Drain.

TIP

OATMEAL MUFFINS

	IMPERIAL	METRIC
eggs; beaten	2 medium	2 medium
brown sugar	2/3 cup	150 mL
oil	1/2 cup	125 mL
buttermilk (see * p.194)	1/2 cup	125 mL
flour	1 cup	250 mL
rolled oats	2/3 cup	150 mL
baking powder	1 tsp.	5 mL
baking soda	1/2 tsp.	2 mL
salt	1/2 tsp.	2 mL
brown sugar	1/2 cup	125 mL
walnuts; chopped	1/4 cup	50 mL
cinnamon	1 tsp.	5 mL

1: Beat together eggs, sugar, oil & milk.

2: Stir in flour, oats, baking powder, soda & salt. Let stand 5 minutes.

3: Spoon batter into paper-lined muffin cups.

4: Mix brown sugar, nuts & cinnamon. Sprinkle on top of muffins.

5: For 6 muffins, bake 1 1/2-2 minutes on full power.

* Remember... if you don't have a full tray for your last batch, they won't take the full cooking time!

BREAKFAST MUFFINS

-One of my favourites!

	IMPERIAL	METRIC
brown sugar	½ cup	125 mL
butter or margarine	¼ cup	50 mL
egg ; beaten	1 medium	1 medium
carrot ; shredded	1	1
buttermilk (see ✱ p.194)	½ cup	125 mL
flour	¾ cup	175 mL
granola	½ cup	125 mL
baking powder	1 tsp.	5 mL
salt	¼ tsp.	1 mL
baking soda	¼ tsp.	1 mL

1: Beat together sugar, butter, egg, carrot & buttermilk.

2: Mix in flour, granola, baking powder, salt & soda. Spoon batter into paper-lined muffin cups, after sitting 5 min.

3: For 6 muffins, bake 2-3 minutes on full power. (Remember, if you don't have a full tray of muffins, it will take less cooking time.)

TIP

Make your own granola (see P. 235) & your own granola bars too (see P. 181)

PUMPKIN MUFFINS

	IMPERIAL	METRIC
pumpkin; cooked	1 cup	250 mL
sugar	1 cup	250 mL
oil	1 cup	250 mL
buttermilk (see * p.194)	½ cup	125 mL
eggs	2 medium	2 medium
flour	1⅔ cups	400 mL
walnuts	1 cup	250 mL
pumpkin pie spice	2 tsp.	10 mL
baking soda	1 tsp.	5 mL
salt	½ tsp.	2 mL

1: Beat together pumpkin, sugar, oil, buttermilk & eggs.

2: Add flour, nuts, spice, soda & salt.

3: Let batter sit for 5-10 minutes ... as you do for all cakes & muffins. (See P. 159)

4: Pour into paper-lined muffin cups. Bake 3-4½ minutes on full power for 6 muffins.

TIP

Just for a change, I sometimes put a frosting on these & serve as cupcakes.

DREAM CAKE

-Another one of my Mother's recipes ... very rich ... but great for a shower or tea party!

	IMPERIAL	METRIC
butter	½ cup	125 mL
brown sugar	½ cup	125 mL
flour	1½ cups	375 mL
eggs	3 medium	3 medium
brown sugar	1½ cups	375 mL
flour	3 tbsp.	50 mL
baking powder	½ tsp.	2 mL
salt	¼ tsp.	1 mL
vanilla	1 tsp.	5 mL
glazed cherries; chopped	½ cup	125 mL
walnuts; chopped	½ cup	125 mL

1: Soften ½ cup (125 mL) butter 30-45 seconds, then blend with ½ cup (125 mL) of brown sugar & 1½ cups (375 mL) of flour.

2: Press into the bottom of an 8" x 12" (20 cm x 30 cm) pan. Bake uncovered, 4-5 minutes on full power.

3: Beat eggs until foamy, then blend in remaining brown sugar & flour, baking powder, salt & vanilla.

4: Stir in cherries & nuts. Pour mixture over crust & bake uncovered, 9-11 minutes on full power.

5: Allow to cool. If desired, top with butter icing (P. 210)

DR. M°GONIGLE'S LEMON CAKE

- Dr M°Gonigle is a dedicated "microwaver"!
This lemon cake is a favourite.

	IMPERIAL	METRIC
Duncan Hines Lemon Supreme cake mix	1 (19oz.) pkg.	1 (520g) pkg.
lemon Jell-o	1 (3oz.) pkg.	1 (85g) pkg.
oil	½ cup	125 mL
water	¾ cup	175 mL
eggs; beaten	4 medium	4 medium

1: Beat together cake mix, Jell-o, oil, water & eggs.
2: Let stand 5-10 minutes. (see P. 159)
3: Pour into a microwave bundt pan & place on a meat rack in the oven.
4: Bake uncovered, 8-10 minutes on full power. Test with a toothpick.

TIP

If you don't wish to frost this cake; grease & sprinkle graham wafer crumbs in pan, shake out excess crumbs, pour batter in pan & bake.

LINDA'S CHOCOLATE CAKE

- Delicious ... especially with "gooey" chocolate icing!

	IMPERIAL	METRIC
flour	2 cups	500 mL
sugar	I cup	250 mL
cocoa	¼ cup	50 mL
baking powder	I tsp.	5 mL
baking soda	½ tsp.	2 mL
salt	½ tsp.	2 mL
mayonnaise	½ cup	125 mL
water	I cup	250 mL
vanilla	I tsp.	5 mL

1: Combine flour, sugar, cocoa, baking powder, soda & salt. Let stand 5 min.
2: Blend in mayonnaise, water & vanilla. Mix well.
3: Lightly grease a 6"x 10" (1.5 L) baking dish & pour in cake mixture.
4: Place on a meat rack & bake 6-8 minutes on full power. Test with a toothpick.
5: Frost with chocolate icing or top with cherry pie filling when cooled.

ZUCCHINI CAKE

-Another favorite & it's GOT to be good for you!

	IMPERIAL	METRIC
eggs	3 medium	3 medium
sugar	2½ cups	625 mL
oil	¾ cup	175 mL
zucchini ; grated	1½ cups	375 mL
flour	2½ cups	625 mL
salt	1 tsp.	5 mL
baking powder	¼ tsp.	1 mL
baking soda	1½ tsp.	7 mL
cinnamon	1 tbsp.	15 mL
cloves	½ tsp.	2 mL
vanilla	1 tsp.	5 mL
chopped nuts	¾ cup	175 mL

1: Blend eggs, sugar, oil & zucchini. Mix well.
2: Mix in flour, salt, baking powder, soda, cinnamon, cloves & vanilla. Mix well.
3: Stir in chopped nuts. Let the batter sit 5-10 minutes (see P. 159)
4: Pour into bundt pan or ring mold. Place pan on a meat rack.
5: Bake uncovered, 10-12 minutes on full power. Test with a toothpick, then let stand 10 minutes "carry-over cooking time." Cool & frost.

CHOCOLATE ZUCCHINI CAKE

- Delicious!

1: Make zucchini cake as per previous page, but OMIT the cinnamon & cloves & replace with ½ cup (125 mL) of cocoa.
2: Bake uncovered, 8-10 minutes on full power. This cake cooks faster than regular zucchini cake because of added dry ingredients.

TAMMY'S WHIPPED FROSTING

- A nice light topping for a cake.

	IMPERIAL	METRIC
whipping cream	1 pint	500 mL
instant pudding	1 (4 oz.) pkg.	1 (113 g) pkg.
milk	1 cup	250 mL

1: Whip cream, stir in pudding & milk, & it's ready for that special occasion.

Refrigerate or freeze left-over frosting until needed again. Soften 30 seconds - 1 minute on full power.

TIP

CARROT CAKE

- Just think ... this would take 1 hour in a conventional oven!

	IMPERIAL	METRIC
eggs	3 medium	3 medium
sugar	1½ cups	375 mL
oil	1 cup	250 mL
vanilla	1 tsp.	5 mL
carrots ; grated	2½ cups	625 mL
flour	1½ cups	375 mL
salt	½ tsp.	2 mL
baking soda	1¼ tsp.	6 mL
cinnamon	2½ tsp.	12 mL
ground cloves	1¼ tsp.	6 mL
raisins	¾ cup	175 mL
walnuts ; chopped	¾ cup	175 mL

1: Beat together eggs, sugar, oil, vanilla, & carrots.

2: Mix in flour, salt, soda, cinnamon & cloves. Let stand 5 minutes.

3: Plump raisins by placing in a bowl with 1 cup (250 mL) of water & cook 1½-2 minutes on full power. Let stand 1 minute & then drain.

4: Fold plumped raisins & walnuts into the cake batter.

5: Let batter sit 5-10 minutes. (see P. 159)

6: Pour batter into bundt pan or ring mold. Place on a meat rack & cook

uncovered, 12-14 minutes on full power.
Test with a toothpick.

7:   Let stand 10 minutes "carry-over cooking time." This is really nice with cream cheese frosting or just sliced & buttered!

Cupcakes in cones:
- use your favorite cake mix (cut back liquid by ¼ if it's a runny mix.)
- spoon batter into flat-bottomed cones (½ full) & cook 20-25 seconds each on full power.
- GREAT for kids' parties ...top with ice cream or frosting & decorate with candy or raisins!

TIP

JAN'S WHITE CAKE

–This makes a nice 2-layer cake & goes well with "Tammy's Whipped Frosting" P. 203

	IMPERIAL	METRIC
flour	2 cups	500 mL
sugar	1½ cups	375 mL
baking powder	3½ tsp.	17 mL
salt	1 tsp.	5 mL
shortening	½ cup	125 mL
milk	1 cup	250 mL
vanilla	1 tsp.	5 mL
egg whites ; beaten	4 medium	4 medium

1: Combine all ingredients, except egg whites, in a mixing bowl. Beat on high speed for 2 minutes.

2: Fold in egg whites & beat another 2 minutes.

3: Pour into 2 cake pans. Let stand 5 minutes, allowing the leavening agent to start working.

4: Place cake on a meat rack & bake 1 layer at a time. Bake each layer 4-5 minutes on full power. Test with a toothpick. Let stand 5-10 minutes.

TIP

Wax paper in the bottom of each cake pan makes for ease turning them out.

STEAMED CARROT PUDDING

-A Christmas tradition!

	IMPERIAL	METRIC
flour	2 cups	500 mL
brown sugar	1 cup	250 mL
baking soda	1 tsp.	5 mL
cinnamon	1 tsp.	5 mL
nutmeg	1 tsp.	5 mL
salt	½ tsp.	2 mL
cloves ; ground	¼ tsp.	1 mL
raisins	1 cup	250 mL
mixed candied fruit	1 cup	250 mL
nuts; chopped	½ cup	125 mL
carrots ; grated	1½ cups	375 mL
orange juice	⅔ cup	150 mL
oil	½ cup	125 mL
egg	1 medium	1 medium

1: Mix all ingredients in a large bowl & let stand 5 minutes.

2: Pour into a lightly-greased bundt or tube pan. Cover with plastic wrap. (This is how it's steamed!)

3: Cook 9-11 minutes on full power. Let stand 10 minutes "carry-over cooking time."

4: Invert onto a serving plate & serve with Hot Butter Sauce (P. 210) or Linda's Lemon Sauce (P. 211)

ISABEL'S DARK FRUIT CAKE

-Isabel's enthusiasm for microwaving led us to this "fabulous" fruit cake !

	IMPERIAL	METRIC
blanched almonds	1 lb.	500 g
pecans	1 lb.	500 g
juice of 1 orange		
raisins	4 lbs.	2 kg
mixed fruit	1 lb.	500 g
candied cherries	1 lb.	500 g
dates	1 lb.	500 g
grape juice	1 cup	250 mL
flour	4 cups	1 L
butter	1 lb.	500 g.
white sugar	2 cups	500 mL
OR brown sugar	OR 3½ cups	OR 875 mL
eggs; yolks/whites beaten separately	12 med.	12 med.
grape jelly	1(8 oz.) jar	1(250 mL) jar
chocolate; melted	2 tbsp.	25 mL
baking powder	1 tsp.	5 mL

1: Soak nuts overnight in orange juice & the fruit overnight in grape juice.
2: Sprinkle a little of the flour over fruit.
3: Cream butter & sugar together. Remember; you can soften butter 45 seconds - 1 minute on full power, if the butter has come straight out of the refrigerator. (of course remove the foil wrapper first !!)

4: Add beaten egg yolks, grape jelly & melted chocolate. (Melt chocolate 30-45 seconds on full power.)

5: Add baking powder & sifted flour.

6: Add fruit, a small amount at a time, mixing well after each addition

7: Add nuts in the same manner.

8: Fold in stiffly-beaten egg whites.

9: Pour into loaf pans, lined with wax paper. Bake 2 loaves at a time for 18-20 minutes on ½ power (power level 5 or medium). Let stand 10 minutes.

* This recipe will make 6 or 7 loaves. If you have an "extra" loaf to bake alone, decrease baking time to 10-12 minutes on ½ power.

* You'll get more juice from an orange or lemon by first cooking 30-45 seconds on full power.

OATMEAL CAKE

	IMPERIAL	METRIC
rolled oats	1 cup	250 mL
water	1½ cups	375 mL
butter or margarine ; softened	½ cup	125 mL
sugar	1 cup	250 mL
brown sugar	1 cup	250 mL
eggs ; beaten	2 medium	2 medium
flour	1½ cups	375 mL
baking soda	1 tsp.	5 mL
cinnamon	1 tsp.	5 mL
salt	½ tsp.	2 mL
nutmeg	½ tsp.	2 mL

1: Combine oats & water in a batter bowl & cook uncovered, 3-4 min. on high. Let stand.

2: In another bowl, combine softened butter, sugars, beaten eggs, flour, soda, cinnamon, salt, nutmeg & oatmeal.

3: Pour into an 8" x 12" (2L) baking dish or bundt pan. Cook uncovered, 10-12 min on full power. Spread immediately with:

Topping:

	IMPERIAL	METRIC
brown sugar	¾ cup	175 mL
butter or margarine	⅓ cup	75 mL
milk	2 tbsp.	25 mL
coconut ; flaked	1 cup	250 mL
chopped nuts	½ cup	125 mL

1: Combine all ingredients, cook uncovered, 3-4 min on high. Spread on cake.

BUTTER ICING

	IMPERIAL	METRIC
butter	4 tbsp.	50 mL
icing sugar	2 cups	500 mL
vanilla	½ tsp.	2 mL
milk or cream	3 tbsp.	50 mL

1: Cream butter, add remaining ingredients & spread on cooled cake.

Variation: "Cream Cheese Frosting"

Soften one 8 oz (250 g) pkg. cream cheese 45 seconds - 1½ minutes on ½ power. Add to "Butter Icing" above & spread on cooled cake.

* If you just want to "drizzle" this icing over a cake, cut the recipe in half.

HOT BUTTER SAUCE

	IMPERIAL	METRIC
whipping cream	¾ cup	175 mL
milk	¼ cup	50 mL
sugar	¾ cup	175 mL
butter or margarine	½ cup	125 mL
cornstarch	1½ tsp.	7 mL
vanilla	1 tsp.	5 mL

1: Combine whipping cream, milk, sugar, butter & cornstarch in a batter bowl.
2: Cook uncovered, 4-5 minutes on full power, until mixture boils. Boil for 1 minute.
3: Stir in vanilla & serve.

LINDA'S LEMON SAUCE

- Linda made this along with our "CARROT PUDDING", until it became a tradition!

	IMPERIAL	METRIC
brown sugar	1½ cups	375 mL
corn syrup	⅔ cup	150 mL
butter or margarine	½ cup	125 mL
lemon rind; grated	1 lemon	1 lemon
coffee cream	½ cup	125 mL
salt	½ tsp.	2 mL
lemon juice	1 lemon	1 lemon

1: Combine all ingredients in a heat-proof glass mixing bowl. Boil until mixture forms a ball when dropped in cold water. Remove from heat & cool.

2: Add cream, salt & juice. Serve hot with "Carrot Pudding." (P. 207)

MICRO NOTES

Eggs

Cook bacon on a meat rack, to collect drippings, <u>or</u> on paper towel. Always cover with paper towel when cooking, to collect the spatters. Cook bacon on high.

Bacon takes about 1 minute/slice to do, but you'll find the cooking time really depends on the brand of bacon:
a) Thick-sliced takes longer than thin-sliced.
b) The higher the sugar content, the faster it will cook.

Remember:
It is better to <u>undercook</u> & add more time if needed, BUT, once it's overdone it's too late!! ☹

TIP

See P. 10 for "meat rack"

SAUSAGES

These are best done on a browning grill, a dish designed to get HOT in the microwave oven. This is the only way they'll get brown.

Pierce the skin as you do for baked potatoes & cook on full power.

	BROWNING GRILL	MEAT RACK
2 sausages	1-1½ minutes	2-2½ minutes
1 lb. (½ kg)	4-5 minutes	7-8 minutes

After cooking, let stand 3-5 minutes "carry-over cooking time."

See P. 9-10 "Browning grill."

TIP

EGGS 217

	IMPERIAL	METRIC
bacon	2 slices	2 slices
egg	1	1
Cheddar cheese, grated	1 tbsp.	15 mL

1: Cook bacon between 2 pieces of paper towel for 1-1½ minutes on full power. (I find it easier to have a dinner plate under this when cooking ... clean-up is easier, as the plate can go in the dishwasher & the oven floor stays clean!)

2: Crumble bacon into a small custard cup or cereal bowl. Add the egg & pierce the yolk twice with the tines of a fork ... if you're careful, the yolk will not break, but piercing that outer membrane will allow a "steam vent" for the rapid speed of cooking.

3: Sprinkle cheese on the egg & cook covered (with plastic wrap), 1-1½ minutes on power level 6 (medium-high). Let stand until desired doneness.

SCRAMBLED EGGS

#of eggs	Butter	Milk	Cooking time
1	1 tsp. (5 mL)	1 tbsp. (15 mL)	45 sec.- 1 min.
2	2 tsp. (10 mL)	2 tbsp. (30 mL)	1½ - 1¾ min.
4	4 tsp. (20 mL)	4 tbsp. (60 mL)	2½ - 3 min.
6	6 tsp. (30 mL)	6 tbsp. (90 mL)	3½ - 4¼ min.

1: Blend butter, milk & eggs together. Add salt & pepper to taste.

2: Cook, covered, on full power, stirring 2-3 times.

*Eggs will look slightly moist, BUT will finish cooking during standing time.

If you're following a microwave recipe & it doesn't tell you to "cover", you can assume to cook it "uncovered." If it says to cover, then use the casserole lid or plastic wrap. Use wax paper or paper towel if the recipe states it. (See P. 11-14)

TIP

FRIED EGG

- You MUST use a browning grill !

1: Preheat browning grill by placing in the microwave oven, empty, on full power as directions for your grill state. This will be anywhere from 1½ minutes for a small browning dish, to 3-4 minutes for larger ones.
* You will not damage your oven with this "empty" dish as the radiowaves are attracted to the special coating of tin oxide on the bottom. The dish will get VERY HOT & can now be used as a skillet.

2: Add butter or bacon fat to the hot dish & then break your egg or eggs into the dish. * You must puncture the yolk(s) with the tines of a fork.

3: Allow 30-45 seconds / egg on power level 6 (medium - medium high) when using a hot grill.

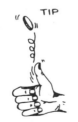

TIP

Heat your grapefruit in the morning, 30-45 seconds on full power!

HAM & EGG BAKE

- Great on toast or for sandwiches!

	IMPERIAL	METRIC
eggs	8 medium	8 medium
milk	½ cup	125 mL
salad dressing	½ cup	125 mL
pimiento ; chopped	¼ cup	50 mL
green pepper; chopped	¼ cup	50 mL
cooked ham ; cubed	1 cup	250 mL
salt	1 tsp.	5 mL
tomato; chopped	1	1

1: Beat together eggs, milk & salad dressing.

2: Stir in pimiento, green pepper, ham & salt.

3: Cook in a covered casserole, 4-5 minutes on full power, stirring 2-3 times.

4: Stir in tomato. Let stand 3 minutes "carry-over cooking time", & serve.

Bake your eggs for sandwiches or salads in a muffin pan!

TIP

OMELETTE

	IMPERIAL	METRIC
eggs	3 medium	3 medium
milk	3 tbsp.	50 mL
salt	½ tsp.	2 mL
pepper	⅛ tsp.	0.5 mL
butter	1 tbsp.	15 mL

1: Beat together eggs, milk, salt & pepper.
2: Melt butter in a glass pie plate for 30-45 seconds on full power.
3: Pour the egg mixture into the plate & cook covered, 1½-2 minutes on full power
4: Lift cooked edges to the center with a spatula & allow the uncooked center to flow to the outside edges. Cook covered, another 1-1½ minutes on ½ power. Let stand 1-2 minutes "carry-over cooking time."

VARIATION:

At this point you may sprinkle on top:

cooked crumbled bacon- 1-1½ min /slice on full power

sautéed green pepper - 1½-2 min/ ½ cup in butter

sautéed mushrooms - 1½- 2 min/ ½ cup no butter

sautéed onions - 1½- 2 min/ ½ cup in butter

grated Cheddar cheese - to taste

5: Sprinkle one or all of these toppings on your omelette, reserving a small amount for a topping.

6: Carefully fold omelette in half with a spatula. Sprinkle remaining topping on for a garnish. Let stand for 1-2 minutes longer. Heat covered with wax paper, 30 sec. on full power.

OATMEAL

- No more pots to scrub ... no more mess!

	IMPERIAL	METRIC
oatmeal	1/3 cup	75 mL
water	2/3 cup	150 mL

1: Combine oatmeal & water in a bowl & cook 1½-2 minutes on full power.

2: Let stand 1 minute for "regular" & 3-4 minutes for "old fashioned."

Make this right in the bowl! ... for more than one bowl, increase your cooking time.

"O" TIP

QUICHE LORRAINE

-This makes a really nice luncheon
served with a tossed salad.

	IMPERIAL	METRIC
bacon	8 slices	8 slices
onion; finely chopped	¼ cup	50 mL
Swiss cheese ; grated	1½ cups	375 mL
baked pastry shell (P. 160)	8"	20 cm
eggs	3 medium	3 medium
cream	1 cup	250 mL
salt	½ tsp.	2 mL
basil	½ tsp.	2 mL
nutmeg	¼ tsp.	1 mL

1: Arrange bacon on a meat rack & cover
with paper towel. Cook 5-6 minutes
on full power.

2: Sprinkle crumbled bacon, onion &
cheese in the bottom of a baked pastry shell.

3: Blend eggs, cream, salt & basil. Pour
over bacon mixture. Sprinkle with
nutmeg & cook 6-8 minutes on full
power. Let stand 10 minutes "carry-
over cooking time."

Miscellaneous

WHITE SAUCE

	IMPERIAL	METRIC
butter	2 tbsp.	25 mL
flour	2 tbsp.	25 mL
salt	½ tsp.	2 mL
pepper	⅛ tsp.	0.5 mL
milk	1 cup	250 mL

1: Combine all ingredients & heat 3-4 minutes on full power, until thickened.

CHEESE SAUCE

	IMPERIAL	METRIC
white sauce	as above	as above
mustard	¼ tsp.	1 mL
sharp Cheddar cheese; grated	¾ cup	175 mL

1: Make white sauce (above) & add mustard & cheese. Stir until cheese is melted.

* Leftover sauces reheat beautifully in the microwave oven.

MOCK GRAPE JELLY

-This is from Denise in Winnipeg. It makes great jelly!

	IMPERIAL	METRIC
beet water <u>or</u> juice	3 cups	750 mL
Certo crystals	1 (2 oz.) box	1 (57g) box
sugar	4 cups	1 L
lemon juice	2 tsp.	10 mL
grape <u>OR</u> raspberry Jell-o	1 (6 oz.) pkg.	1 (170g) pkg.

1: Combine beet water & Certo. Bring to a boil; 6-8 minutes on full power.

2: Add sugar & lemon juice & boil for 10 minutes more, stirring 2 or 3 times.

Remember:
> When your liquid reaches a boil again, turn the power level down to 7 or 8, to maintain a rolling boil without boiling over.

3: Add Jell-o & stir well.

4: Skim off foam from the top & pour into hot sterilized jars.

5: Seal with paraffin.

TIP

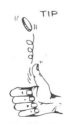

Unfortunately, you <u>CANNOT</u> melt paraffin in the microwave oven as it has no moisture in it!

STRAWBERRY RHUBARB JAM

	IMPERIAL	METRIC
strawberries	1½ pints	750 mL
rhubarb ; sliced	2 cups	500 mL
powdered pectin	1(2 oz.) pkg.	1(57g) pkg.
sugar	4 cups	1 L

1: Combine strawberries & rhubarb in a covered 2 qt (2L) casserole. Cook 5-7 minutes on full power.

2: Stir in pectin & cook uncovered, 3½-4½ minutes on full power.

3: Stir in sugar & cook uncovered, 3-4 minutes on full power (until it boils 1 full minute.)

4: Pour into hot sterilized jars & seal with paraffin. (You cannot melt paraffin in the microwave oven. See P. 227)

CRAN-APPLE JELLY

-Jams & jellies are so easy in the micro-wave oven as there's no scorching!

	IMPERIAL	METRIC
cranberry juice	2½ cups	625 mL
apple juice	1½ cups	375 mL
powdered pectin	1 (2 oz.) pkg.	1 (57g) pkg.
sugar	4 cups	1 L

1: Combine cranberry juice, apple juice & pectin in a covered 2qt (2L) casserole. Cook 11-13 minutes on full power, stirring once or twice.

2: Stir in sugar & cook uncovered, 10-12 minutes on full power (until it boils 1 full minute.)

3: Pour into hot sterilized jars & seal with paraffin. (You cannot melt paraffin in the microwave oven. See P. 227)

You can warm your baby's bottle in the microwave oven too! Heat 30-45 seconds on full power.

TIP

ZUCCHINI JAM

- A great way to use up all those extra zucchini from the garden!

	IMPERIAL	METRIC
zucchini	6 cups	1.5 L
sugar	6 cups	1.5 L
crushed pineapple ; with juice	1 cup	250 mL
lemon juice	½ cup	125 mL
apricot Jell-o	1 (6 oz.) pkg.	1 (170 g) pkg.

1: Peel zucchini, cut out pulp & cut into cubes. Cook in a large covered casserole 15-20 minutes on full power.

2: Add sugar, pineapple (& juice), & lemon juice. Boil hard for 15-20 minutes.

3: Add Jell-o & stir well until dissolved. Pour into hot sterilized jars & seal with paraffin. (You cannot melt paraffin in the microwave oven. See P.227)

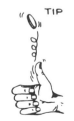
TIP

This jam will take 2 days to set.

LITA'S SPONGE CANDY

	IMPERIAL	METRIC
sugar	1 cup	250 mL
dark corn syrup	1 cup	250 mL
vinegar	1 tbsp.	15 mL
soda	1 tbsp.	15 mL

1: Combine sugar, syrup & vinegar in a covered 2qt (2L) casserole. Cook 3-4 minutes on full power.

2: Uncover, & cook another 5-10 minutes, or until it reaches a "brittle" stage when a small amount is dropped in cold water.

3: Quickly stir in soda. (The mixture will foam up.)

4: Pour into a buttered, foil-lined 8" (20cm) square pan. Let stand to cool. Remove from pan & break into serving pieces.

TIP

Warm your brandy 30-45 seconds/glass. (Remember... gold trim is a no-no!)

YOGURT

-A quick & easy way to make your own "homemade yogurt."

	IMPERIAL	METRIC
non-fat dry milk crystals	1½ cups	375 mL
milk	1 cup	250 mL
evaporated milk	1(5.3oz.) can	1(148g) can
plain yogurt	⅓ cup	75 mL

1: Combine crystals with enough water to make 2 cups. Stir in milk & cook 6-8 minutes on full power.

2: Stir in evaporated milk & cool to 115° using a cooking thermometer.

3: Mix a small amount of milk mixture with the yogurt, then pour all into mixture & stir well.

4: Cook, covered with plastic wrap, on the defrost cycle for 1½-2½ minutes OR back to 115°. Don't stir ; but let the mixture sit in the microwave oven, undisturbed for 1-1½ hours. By this time the temperature of the yogurt drops.

5: Cook another 1½-2½ minutes on the defrost cycle & let sit again.

 * You must maintain the yogurt at a temperature of 110°-115° for a total of 3 hours from start to finish. Chill.

* If your microwave oven will hold anything at a given temperature, use that setting .... Set the temperature for 115° & leave for 3 hours. EASY ?

* Use yogurt to replace sour cream for less calories.

* Serve yogurt as a pudding.

* Mix yogurt with fruit, honey or jam

* Serve yogurt with granola or pies

and .... it's good for you!

Warm baby food easily... remove the lid from the jar & heat 25-30 seconds on full power.

TIP

MISC.

CHESTNUTS

♪ " Chestnuts roasting on an open fire ?.. "
& no more fuss!

1: Cut an "x" into the sides of the
shells & cook 1½-2 minutes/dozen
on full power. Now that's easy!!

HOT MULLED WINE

- Great after skiing!

	IMPERIAL	METRIC
apple cider	3 cups	750 mL
sugar	¼ cup	50 mL
cinnamon sticks	3	3
whole cloves	6	6
lemon ; sliced	½	½
orange ; sliced	½	½
dry wine ; red or white	1 bottle	1 bottle

1: Combine all ingredients, except wine,
& boil until sugar dissolves. Cook another 10 minutes. Let stand 10 minutes
"carry-over cooking time."
2: Stir in the bottle of wine & serve.

* "Guaranteed to warm the cockles of
your heart!"

HOT SANDWICHES

Wrap your sandwich in paper towel & heat 20-45 seconds on full power.(Don't use plastic wrap as it will leave it damp!)

Put open-faced sandwiches on a meat rack OR on paper towel,& heat 20-45 seconds on full power.

* Remember, cheese is very delicate in the microwave oven. Overcooking will leave it rubbery. For cheese toppings on casseroles or snack toppings ; add the cheese towards the end of the cooking time.

HOT DOGS

One raw wiener in a bun, wrapped in a napkin, will take 25-35 sec. on full power.

One frozen wiener & bun, wrapped in a napkin, will take 1 minute on full power.

½ dozen hot dogs , wrapped in a napkin, will take 2-3 minutes on full power.

* Prepare a bunch of these for the freezer & place in freezer bags. After school the kids can grab one & cook it for a quick snack!

HOT CHOCOLATE

	IMPERIAL	METRIC
cocoa	1 tsp.	5 mL
white sugar	2 tsp.	10 mL
milk	1 cup	250 mL

1: Combine dry ingredients in a mug. Blend with the back of a spoon.
2: Stir in milk. (Don't worry, the lumps will disappear !!) ☺
3: Heat 1½ minutes/mug on full power.

HOT COFFEE

Make your coffee right in the mug... boil the water 2-3 minutes & add 1 tsp. (5 mL) of instant coffee. You can refrigerate left-over coffee if it hasn't sat too long. Take it out & heat it in your mug 2-3 minutes on full power.

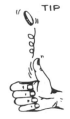

TIP "Label" leftover coffee in the refrigerator! One sleepy morning Doug drank a mouthful of his coffee, & to his "aghast" found it was my teriyaki sauce! What a rude awakening! ☹

GRANOLA

- A filling & nutritious breakfast... also great on ice cream or desserts.

	IMPERIAL	METRIC
oat flakes; or rolled oats	4 cups	1 L
wheat flakes	1 cup	250 mL
coconut	1 cup	250 mL
walnuts	½ cup	125 mL
sunflower or sesame seeds	½ cup	125 mL
brown sugar	½ cup	125 mL
honey	½ cup	125 mL
oil	½ cup	125 mL
salt	½ tsp.	2 mL
vanilla	1 tsp.	5 mL
raisins	1 cup	250 mL

1: Combine all ingredients, except the raisins. Cook uncovered, 10 minutes on full power, stirring 3 or 4 times.

2: Stir in raisins & cook another 2 minutes. Cool & store in an airtight container. Serve as a dry cereal.

* For a "multi-grain" cereal, combine: oat flakes, rye flakes & barley flakes to make 4 cups (1 L).

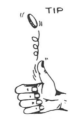
TIP

Make your own granola bars ... see P. 181

see P. 181

DRIED HERBS

- So easy to have your own herbs ... try this with celery leaves, mint, parsley etc.

1: Wash & pat dry.
2: Arrange between paper towels & heat 2-4 minutes on full power.
3: Let stand on the counter, uncovered, until cool & dry.

DRIED FLOWERS

- Some dry better than others... half-opened are best.

1: Half-fill a glass baking dish with silica gel.
2: Arrange flowers (stem down into gel) & gently sprinkle remaining gel over flowers.
3: Place baking dish in the microwave oven with a cup of water in the corner.
4: Heat 1-2 minutes on full power. Let stand overnight & remove flowers gently.

PLAY DOH

- Fun for the kids!

Children love to cook like Mommy & play doh has an added attraction .... they can poke it, roll it, squish it & some even try to eat it BUT discover it's too salty!!

	IMPERIAL	METRIC
flour	2 cups	500 mL
salt	1 cup	250 mL
alum	1 tbsp.	15 mL
water	2 cups	500 mL
oil	1 tbsp.	15 mL
food coloring	- as desired -	

1: Mix the dry ingredients, then blend in the wet. A food processor works great for this.

2: Cook 4-6 minutes on full power. Cool.

* This will keep several weeks in the refrigerator.

* You can even bake their "creations" in a slow oven or microwave oven. Place on cardboard or a meat rack & bake on the defrost cycle for 45 sec.-1 min. per piece. Cool & dry on counter.

* For several colours; mix up plain, divide into sections & colour.

INDEX

INDEX

INDEX

INDEX

INDEX

INDEX

INDEX

MICRO NOTES

-

MICRO NOTES

"HELPFUL TIMINGS"

From "WELCOME TO MICROWAVE COOKING" by Susan Calder

Here are some basic timings.... all are on full power unless stated otherwise.

Apple; baked	2-2½ min./apple (cover)
Baby bottle; each	30-45 sec.
Bacon	½-1½ min./slice
Baked potato	4-6 min./potato
Butter; melted	45 sec.-1 min./ ¼ lb.
Butter; softened	10-15 sec./¼ lb.
Casseroles; cooked ingredients	8-10 min./2qt (2L) size
Cocoa	1½-2 min./mug
Coffee; instant	2-2½ min./cup
Corn on the cob; in husk or wrapped	2-3 min./cob
Dinner plate; reheat	1-2 min. (covered)
Dinner plate; cold → reheat	2½-3½ min.(Level 8: med.high)
Dinner rolls; in paper towel	10-15 sec. each
Dinner rolls; basket & paper towel	30-45 sec./ ½ dozen
Egg (1)	1-1½ min (Level 8: med. high)
Fish	4 min./lb. (6-8 min./kg.)
Ground beef	4-6 min./lb. (9-13 min./kg)
Hot dog; wiener & bun in napkin	25-35 sec. each
Muffin	10-15 sec. each
Pie	30-45 sec. each
Sandwich; in paper towel	30-45 sec. each
Soup	1½-2 min./bowl
Vegetables; above-ground	6-8 min./lb. (10-12 min./kg)
Vegetables; root (with ¼ cup water)	
Vegetables; canned (drain)	1-2 min./cup
Vegetables; blanched (covered)	3-4 min/lb (6-8 min./kg)
Water; boiling	2-3 min./cup

"HELPFUL TIMINGS"

From "WELCOME TO MICROWAVE COOKING" by Susan Calder

Here are some basic timings .... all are on full power unless stated otherwise.

Apple; baked. . . . . 2-2½ min./apple (cover)
Baby bottle; each . . . . 30-45 sec.
Bacon . . . . ½-1½ min./slice
Baked potato. . . . . 4-6 min./potato
Butter; melted. . . . . 45 sec.-1 min./ ¼ lb.
Butter; softened . . . . 10-15 sec./¼ lb.
Casseroles; cooked ingredients. . . 8-10 min./2qt (2L) size
Cocoa.. . . . . 1½-2 min./mug
Coffee; instant. . . . . 2-2½ min./cup
Corn on the cob; in husk or wrapped. . . 2-3 min./cob
Dinner plate; reheat . . . . 1-2 min. (covered)
Dinner plate; cold→reheat . . . . 2½-3½ min.(Level 8: med. high)
Dinner rolls; in paper towel. . . . 10-15 sec. each
Dinner rolls; basket & paper towel .30-45 sec./ ½ dozen
Egg (1). . . . . 1-1½ min(Level 8: med. high)
Fish.. . . . . .4 min./lb. (6-8 min./kg.)
Ground beef. . . . . .4-6 min./lb. (9-13 min./kg)
Hot dog; wiener & bun in napkin . . 25-35 sec. each
Muffin. . . . . 10-15 sec. each
Pie . . . . 30-45 sec. each
Sandwich; in paper towel. . . . . . 30-45 sec. each
Soup.. . . . . 1½-2 min./bowl
Vegetables; above-ground. . . . . . }
Vegetables; root (with ¼ cup water)} 6-8 min./lb. (10-12 min./kg)
Vegetables; canned (drain). . . . . 1-2 min./cup
Vegetables; blanched (covered). . . 3-4 min/lb(6-8 min./kg)
Water; boiling. . . . . 2-3 min./cup

For more copies of "WELCOME TO MICROWAVE COOKING", please send cheque or money order to: SUSAN CALDER

942 TUXEDO PLACE

VICTORIA, B.C.   V8X 4T2

Order 5 books get 1 free.

- -

Please send __ copies of " WELCOME TO MICROWAVE COOKING", at $12.95 per copy, plus $1.50 for handling. (total order). I am enclosing $____.

Name : _____

Address:_____

_____ Postal Code:_____

U.S. orders payable in U.S. funds.

═══

For more copies of "WELCOME TO MICROWAVE COOKING", please send cheque or money order to: SUSAN CALDER

942 TUXEDO PLACE

VICTORIA, B.C.   V8X 4T2

Order 5 books get 1 free.

- -

Please send __ copies of " WELCOME TO MICROWAVE COOKING", at $12.95 per copy, plus $1.50 for handling. (total order). I am enclosing $____.

Name : _____

Address:_____

_____ Postal Code:_____

U.S. orders payable in U.S. funds.